Bond

Verbal Reasoning

Assessment Papers

10–11+ years
Book 1

J M Bond

Nelson Thornes

First published in 1973 by:
Thomas Nelson and Sons Ltd

This edition published in 2012 by:
Nelson Thornes Ltd
Delta Place
27 Bath Road
CHELTENHAM
GL53 7TH
United Kingdom

13 14 / 10 9 8 7 6 5 4 3 2

A catalogue record for this book is available from the British Library

ISBN 978 1 4085 1699 7

Page make-up by Tech Set Ltd

Printed in China by 1010 Printing International Ltd

Before you get started

What is Bond?

This book is part of the Bond Assessment Papers series for verbal reasoning, which provides a **thorough and progressive course in verbal reasoning** from ages six to twelve. It builds up reasoning skills from book to book over the course of the series.

Bond's verbal reasoning resources are ideal preparation for the 11+ and other secondary school selection exams.

How does the scope of this book match real exam content?

Verbal Reasoning 10-11+ Book 1 and *Book 2* are the core Bond 11+ books. Each paper is **pitched at the level of a typical 11+ exam** and practises a wide range of questions drawn from the four distinct groups of verbal reasoning question types: sorting words, selecting words, anagrams, coded sequences and logic. The papers are fully in line with 11+ and other selective exams for this age group but are designed to practise a **wider variety of skills and question types** than most other practice papers so that children are always challenged to think – and don't get bored repeating the same question type again and again. We believe that variety is the key to effective learning. It helps children 'think on their feet' and cope with the unexpected: it is surprising how often children come out of verbal reasoning exams having met question types they have not seen before.

What does the book contain?

- **13 papers** – each one contains 80 questions.
- **Tutorial links throughout** – 📖 – this icon appears in the margin next to the questions. It indicates links to the relevant section in *How to do ...11+ Verbal Reasoning*, our invaluable subject guide that offers explanations and practice for all core question types.
- **Scoring devices** – there are score boxes in the margins and a Progress Chart on page 64. The chart is a visual and motivating way for children to see how they are doing. It also turns the score into a percentage that can help decide what to do next.
- **Next Steps Planner** – advice on what to do after finishing the papers can be found on the inside back cover.
- **Answers** – located in an easily-removed central pull-out section.

How can you use this book?

One of the great strengths of Bond Assessment Papers is their flexibility. They can be used at home, in school and by tutors to:

- **set timed formal practice tests** – allow about 45 minutes per paper in line with standard 11+ demands. Reduce the suggested time limit by five minutes to practise working at speed.

- provide **bite-sized chunks** for regular practice
- **highlight strengths and weaknesses** in the core skills
- identify **individual needs**
- set **homework**
- follow a **complete 11+ preparation strategy** alongside *The Parents' Guide to the 11+* (see below).

It is best to start at the beginning and work through the papers in order. If you are using the book as part of a careful run in to the 11+, we suggest that you also have two other essential Bond resources close at hand:

How to do … 11+ Verbal Reasoning: the subject guide that explains all the question types practised in this book. Use the cross-reference icons to find the relevant sections.

The Parents' Guide to the 11+: the step-by-step guide to the whole 11+ experience. It clearly explains the 11+ process, provides guidance on how to assess children, helps you to set complete action plans for practice and explains how you can use the *Verbal Reasoning 10-11+ Book 1* and *Book 2* as part of a strategic run-in to the exam.

See the inside front cover for more details of these books.

What does a child's score mean and how can it be improved?

It is unfortunately impossible to guarantee that a child will pass the 11+ exam if they achieve a certain score on any practice book or paper. Success on the day depends on a host of factors, including the scores of the other children sitting the test. However, we can give some guidance on what a score indicates and how to improve it.

If children colour in the Progress Chart on page 64, this will give an idea of present performance in percentage terms. The Next Steps Planner inside the back cover will help you to decide what to do next to help a child progress. It is always valuable to go over wrong answers with children. If they are having trouble with any particular question type, follow the tutorial links to *How to do … 11+ Verbal Reasoning* for step-by-step explanations and further practice.

Don't forget the website…!

Visit www.bond11plus.co.uk for lots of advice, information and suggestions on everything to do with Bond, the 11+ and helping children to do their best.

Paper 1

1–5 Look at these groups of words.

A	B	C	D	E
asthma	spotty	fig	celery	mole
flu	freckled	grape	swede	seal

Choose the correct group for each of the words below. Write in the letter.

clear _B_ ✓ sprouts _D_ ✓ fever _A_ ✓ ewe _E_ ✓ currant _C_ ✓ bean _D_ ✓

pony _E_ ✓ tanned _B_ ✓ damson _C_ ✓ cough _A_ ✓

Underline one word in the brackets which is most opposite in meaning to the word in capitals.

Example WIDE (broad most vague long <u>narrow</u> motorway)

6 COOL (<u>warm</u> hot cold icy frozen)

7 OFF-HAND (spontaneous <u>precise</u> casual easygoing forced)

8 SIMPLE (idle comfortable easy soft <u>complicated</u>) ✓

9 ASSIST (<u>hinder</u> help aid handle halt)

10 INITIAL (<u>last</u> early letter name first)

Underline the one word in the brackets which will go equally well with both the pairs of words outside the brackets.

Example rush, attack cost, fee (price, hasten, strike, <u>charge</u>, money)

11 sugar, honey dessert, pudding (meal, cake, <u>sweet</u>, tea, coffee)

12 apartment, rooms level, even (house, bungalow, <u>flat</u>, smooth, straight)

13 speck, stain see, notice (vision, clean, bit, <u>spot</u>, catch)

14 pot, cup attack, beat up (hit, pail, break, pan, <u>mug</u>) ✓

15 pennant, banner tire, exhaust (stone, <u>flag</u>, weary, wilt, sign)

Find the letter which will end the first word and start the second word.

Example peac (<u>h</u>) ome

16 kin (_d_) esk 17 fis (_t_) ool

18 lin (_k_) ind 19 oxe (_n_) ail

20 bor (_e_) ast ✓

Rearrange the muddled letters in capitals to make a proper word. The answer will complete the sentence sensibly.

Example   A BEZAR is an animal with stripes.   ZEBRA ✓

21   For tea we had a lovely AADLS.   SALAD

22   A shape that has three sides is a LETRANIG.   TRIANGLE ✓

23   We sat in a LCERIC.   CIRCLE ✓

24   I like EAASUSGS and chips.   SAUSAGES ✓

25   It gets cold in TRIWEN.   WINTER ✓

Underline two words, one from each group, that go together to form a new word. The word in the first group always comes first.

Example   (hand, <u>green</u>, for)   (light, <u>house</u>, sure)

26   (to, <u>for</u>, has)   (own, many, <u>got</u>) ✓

27   (<u>over</u>, shut, open)   (in, take, torn)

28   (near, after, <u>under</u>)   (some, <u>ground</u>, before)

29   (point, aim, <u>finger</u>)   (side, bottom, <u>print</u>) ✓

30   (am, is, <u>be</u>)   (his, <u>low</u>, high) ✓

Find the four-letter word hidden at the end of one word and the beginning of the next word. The order of the letters may not be changed.

Example   The children had bats and balls   <u>sand</u> ✓

31   They are stored in the shed.   rest ✓

32   Please collect all the books.   tall ✓

33   Sally has gone with the rest.   here ✓

34   It is difficult to concentrate with all this noise.   hall ✓

35   The ship rocks on the rough sea.   hero ✓

Change the first word into the last word, by changing one letter at a time and making a new, different word in the middle.

Example   CASE   <u>CASH</u>   LASH

36   LAND   LEND   LEAD ✓

37   NAIL   BALL   BALL ✓

38   BOOT   HOOT   HOST ✓

39   CAME   COME   COMB ✓

40   SEND   SAND   SANG ✓

Complete the following sentences by selecting the most sensible word from each group of words given in the brackets. Underline the words selected.

> **Example** The (<u>children</u>, books, foxes) carried the (houses, <u>books</u>, steps) home from the (greengrocer, <u>library</u>, factory).

41 The (cats, <u>birds</u>, cows) (<u>flew</u>, burrowed, ran) to their (pool, den, <u>nest</u>).

42 The old lady (jumped, <u>climbed</u>, hopped) on to a (lorry, cycle, <u>bus</u>).

43 Please (colour, <u>check</u>, throw) your (<u>change</u>, book, ball) before you leave the (corridor, bedroom, <u>shop</u>).

44 The (dog, rider, <u>footballer</u>) (jumped, <u>kicked</u>, bit) the ball off the (horse, <u>pitch</u>, garden).

45 (<u>Elephants</u>, rocks, suitcases) have (stony, <u>long</u>, square) (mountains, handles, <u>trunks</u>).

Find and underline the two words which need to change places for each sentence to make sense.

> **Example** She went to <u>letter</u> the <u>write</u>.

46 I <u>there</u> I could go <u>wish</u>.

47 I'll <u>morning</u> up early in the <u>get</u>.

48 <u>Hide</u> did you <u>where</u> the parcel?

49 He found the <u>table</u> on the <u>book</u>.

50 He <u>over</u> the ball <u>threw</u> the wall.

Fill in the missing letters. The alphabet has been written out to help you.

A B C D E F G H I J K L M N O P Q R S T U V W X Y Z

> **Example** AB is to CD as PQ is to <u>RS</u>

51 AC is to BD as MO is to _NP_

52 ACE is to BDF as CEG is to _DFH_

53 AZ is to BY as CX is to _DW_

54 ZX is to VT as SQ is to _OM_

55 AG is to ZT as BH is to _YS_

Fill in the crosswords so that all the given words are included. You have been given one letter as a clue in each crossword.

56–57

t	a	p	e	r
a	■	i	■	i
s	e	e	d	s
t	■	c	■	k
e	v	e	r	y

risky
seeds
every
taste
taper
piece

58–59

b	e	a	r	s
r	■	c	■	u
e	a	t	E	n
a	■	o	■	n
d	i	r	t	y

dirty
eaten
bears
bread
actor
sunny

Give the missing pair of letters in the following sequences. The alphabet has been written out to help you.

A B C D E F G H I J K L M N O P Q R S T U V W X Y Z

Example	CQ	DQ	EP	FP	*GO* ✓
60 AH	BI	CJ	DK		*EL*
61 BA	DC	FE	HG		*JI* ✓
62 ZZA	YBY	XDW	WFU		*VHS* ✓
63 GIH	IKJ	KML	MON		*OQP* ✓

B 23

Underline the two words, one from each group, which are closest in meaning.

Example (race, shop, <u>start</u>) (finish, <u>begin</u>, end)

64 (pale, dark, bulb) (flower, <u>light</u>, day) ✓

65 (leg, <u>weapons</u>, foot) (hands, ankle, <u>arms</u>) ✓

66 (before, connect, <u>right</u>) (<u>correct</u>, wrong, left) ✓

67 (lift, <u>cushion</u>, pillow) (chair, <u>protect</u>, fight) ✓

B 3

68 If the code for TIME is 2786, what does 862 stand for? <u>MET</u> ✓

69–71 If the code for TEASE is 84234, what do the following codes stand for?

284 <u>ATE</u> ✓ 3428 <u>SEAT</u> ✓ 82384 <u>TASTE</u> ✓

72 If the code for PURSE is 96483, what is the code for SUPPER? <u>869934</u> ✓

B 24

Underline the two words which are the odd ones out in the following groups of words.

Example	black	<u>king</u>	purple	green	<u>house</u>
73 stick	pipe	glue	<u>heir</u>	adhere	✓
74 <u>climb</u>	<u>ascend</u>	mountain	hill	cliff	✓
75 <u>arrow</u>	hedgehog	porcupine	<u>pin</u>	needle	
76 attract	enchant	<u>house</u>	charm	<u>bracelet</u>	✓
77 <u>biscuit</u>	flour	sugar	<u>butter</u>	cake	✓

B 4

If A = 1, B = 3, C = 4, D = 5, find the value of:

78 $(C - B) \times D =$ <u>5</u> ✓

79 $(D - A) + (B \times C) =$ <u>28</u> ✓

80 $D - (A + B) =$ <u>1</u> ✓

B 26

very good!

Paper 2

Give the two missing pairs of letters in the following sequences. The alphabet has been written out to help you.

B 23

A B C D E F ⓖ H I J K L M N O ⓟ ⓠ ⓡ S ⓣ U V W X Y Z

	Example	CQ	DQ	EP	FP	*GO* /	*HO*
1	NO	NP	*NQ* ✓	NR	*NS* ✓	NT	
2	JQ	KP	LO	MN	*KM* ✗	*JL* ✗	
3	CN	EP	*GR* ✓	IT	KV	*OZ* ✗	

 3

Here are the number codes for four words. Match the right code to the right word.

B 24

MAST   STAR   REST   TEA

5314   432   7214   1425

4 MAST   *7214* ✗

5 STAR   *1425* ✓

6 REST   ~~*531*~~ *5314* ✓

7 TEA   *432* ✓

8 Write REAM in code.   *9437* ✗

④ 5

Complete the following sentences by selecting the most sensible word from each group of words given in the brackets. Underline the words selected.

B 14

Example   The (<u>children</u>, books, foxes) carried the (houses, <u>books</u>, steps) home from the (greengrocer, <u>library</u>, factory).

9 He painted a (<u>picture</u>, door, dog) which was to hang in the ✓ (garden, street, <u>classroom</u>).

10 She (cooked, blocked, <u>broke</u>) the (<u>vase</u>, salad, weather) which had to be (put to bed, <u>thrown away</u>, bathed).

11 (Caterpillars, flowers, frogs) change into (petals, <u>butterflies</u>, tadpoles) with beautiful (<u>wings</u>, eyes, stems).

12 How many (add, divide, <u>times</u>) do I have to tell (me, <u>you</u>, tales) to close the (sum, sandwich, <u>door</u>) quietly!

13 The sun (<u>rose</u>, violet, tulip) over the horizon like a giant (green, <u>orange</u>, bouncy) (fish, flower, ball).

⑤ 5

Underline two words, one from each group, that go together to form a new word. The word in the first group always comes first.

Example (hand, <u>green</u>, for) (light, <u>house</u>, sure)

14 (rock, face, <u>band</u>) (<u>age</u>, worth, kind) ✓

15 (<u>be</u>, was, do) (age, <u>hind</u>, rear) ✓

16 (life, <u>birth</u>, year) (wrong, <u>day</u>, rear) ✓

17 (silly, jester, <u>fool</u>) (joke, <u>hardy</u>, fair) ✓ *hvmour*

18 (blue, colour, <u>hue</u>) (<u>more</u>, gone, less) ✗

Underline the one word in the brackets which will go equally well with both the pairs of words outside the brackets.

Example rush, attack cost, fee (price, hasten, strike, <u>charge</u>, money)

19 overlook, lose girl, lass (more, <u>miss</u>, mark, drop, lose) ✓

20 bright, well-lit portable, easy to carry (heavy, move, dark, <u>light</u>, glow) ✓

21 cot, cradle copy, forge (<u>crib</u>, bed, stable, zoo, animals) ✓

22 thread, string fasten, tie (lace, <u>needle</u>, pin, wire, bow) ✓

23 timber, pole glimmer, ray (dark, light, shadow, <u>beam</u>, torch) ✓

Find the letter which will end the first word and start the second word.

Example peac (<u>h</u>) ome

24 wis (<u>h</u>) elm ✓

25 boo (<u>k</u>) nee ✓

26 gro (<u>w</u>) ish ✓

27 mea (<u>l</u>) isp ✓

28 sea (<u>t</u>) rap ✓

Rearrange the muddled letters in capitals to make a proper word. The answer will complete the sentence sensibly.

Example A BEZAR is an animal with stripes. ZEBRA

29 NUTMAU is a season of the year. AUTUMN ✓

30 A AONMNIS is a very big house. MANSION ✓

31 It is a big DACORHR with lots of fruit trees. ORCHARD ✓

32 EICCTKR is a team game. CRICKET ✓

33 A RETEFR is a small animal. FERRET ✓

Move one letter from the first word and add it to the second word to make two new words.

Example   hunt   sip   <u>hut</u>   <u>snip</u>

B 13

34   mend   raw   *end*   *warm* ✗

35   plump   and   *pump*   *land* ✓

36   clean   are   *lean*   *care* ✓

37   crave   cat   *cave*   *cart* ✓

38   seal   bride   *sea*   *bridle* ✓   (4) 5

39–43   Look at these headings.

B 1

A	B	C
Musical instruments	Vegetables	Reptiles

Choose the correct group for each of the words below. Write in the letter.

turnip *B* ✓   hugle *A* ✓   adder *C* ✓   drum *A* ✓   cress *B* ✓   snake *C* ✓

piano *A* ✓   onion *B* ✓   tortoise *C* ✓   guitar *A* ✓   (5) 5

Find the three-letter word which can be added to the letters in capitals to make a new word. The new word will complete the sentence sensibly.

B 22

Example   The cat sprang onto the MO.   <u>USE</u>

44   Your front tyre has a CTURE.   *PUN* ✓

45   I have two SQUS and a rectangle.   *ARE* ✓

46   The flowers, which hadn't been WATE, were drooping.   *RED* ✓

47   The washing, which had been BING in the wind, was quite dry.   *LOW* ✓

48   The GER climbed cautiously out of his sett.   *BAD* (5) 5

Find the four-letter word hidden at the end of one word and the beginning of the next word. The order of the letters may not be changed.

B 21

Example   The children had bats and balls.   *sand*

49   There are several pairs of shoes.   *rear* ✓

50   Please climb into the cars now.   *snow* ✓

51   The last three letters are there.   *reel* ✓

52   The question is often asked.   *soft* ✓

53   Soon the play will end.   *lend* ✓   (5) 5

Find and underline the two words which need to change places for each sentence to make sense.

B 17

Example She went to <u>letter</u> the <u>write</u>.

54 Mum was in <u>busy</u> the <u>kitchen</u>.

55 We <u>bus</u> on the last <u>went</u>. ✓

56 You can <u>sums</u> your <u>do</u>. ✓

57 <u>Cold</u> think it is <u>I</u> today. ✓

58 I got <u>my</u> all <u>sums</u> right. ✓

4½ 5

Fill in the crosswords so that all the given words are included. You have been given one letter as a clue in each crossword.

B 19

59–60

b	r	e	a	D
a		x		O
r	e	a	d	S
O		c		e
n	o	t	e	S

notes
reads
bread
doses
baron
exact ✓

61–62

C	o	M	e	S
h		o		p
a	p	p	l	e
l		e		N
r	e	S	e	t

chair
mopes
spent
comes
apple ✓
reset ✓

4 4

Choose two words, one from each set of brackets, to complete the sentences in the best way.

B 15

Example Smile is to happiness as (drink, <u>tear</u>, shout) is to (whisper, laugh, <u>sorrow</u>).

63 Green is to grass as (colour, <u>blue</u>, shade) is to (swim, sand, <u>sky</u>). ✓

64 Food is to hunger as (<u>drink</u>, tea, coffee) is to (<u>thirst</u>, glass, wet). ✓

65 Boy is to man as (<u>girl</u>, pupil, student) is to (school, niece, <u>woman</u>). ✓

66 Top is to bottom as (over, <u>high</u>, aloft) is to (above, upper, <u>low</u>). ✓

67 Well is to ill as (soft, silk, material) is to (<u>heavy</u>, hard, broken). ✗

4 5

Give the two missing numbers in the following sequences.

B 23

Example 2 4 6 8 <u>10</u> <u>12</u>

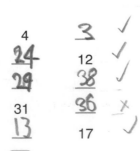

68 18 13 9 6 4 3 ✓

69 72 60 48 36 24 12 ✓

70 3 8 14 21 29 38 ✓

71 7 12 18 25 31 36 ✗

72 11 13 12 15 13 17 ✓

4 5

A and B like blue.

C likes green but not red.

F likes red and green.

E only likes green.

73 Which colour is the most popular? _green_ ✓

74 Which colour is the least popular? _red_ ✓

75 How many more like blue than red? _one_ ✓

76 How many only like one colour? _x̶ 3_ ✗

4

Rearrange the letters in capitals to make another word. The new word has something to do with the first two words.

	Example	spot	soil	SAINT	STAIN
77	brute	savage	BASTE	TASTE ✗
78	curl	circle	POOL	LOOP ✓
79	weak	fragile	FLAIR	FRAIL ✓
80	letter	memo	TONE	NOTE ✓

4

Now go to the Progress Chart to record your score! Total 71 80

Paper 3

If the code for PURCHASE is £ + − × ÷ @ % /, what do these codes stand for?

1 % ÷ @ − / % SHARES   2 % £ − + × / SPRUCE

What are the codes for the following words?

3 ARCHES @−×÷/%   4 SHARP %÷@−£   5 CASH ×@%÷

5

Change one word so that the sentence makes sense. Underline the word you are taking out and write your new word on the line.

Example   I waited in line to buy a book to see the film.   _ticket_

6 After swimming we are sometimes allowed fish and towels for supper. _chips_

7 The artist dipped his brush into the blue cream on his palette. _paint_

8 The train pulled into the supermarket and let the passengers get off. _station_

9 Simon sharpened his ruler over the bin. _pencil_

10 The rain fell heavily against the door pane. _window_

5

Which one letter can be added to the front of all of these words to make new words?

B 12

Example _c_are   _c_at   _c_rate   _c_all

11 _d_ance   _d_ate   _d_ash   _d_art   _d_one

12 _f_are   _f_lag   _f_or   _f_lash   _f_eel

13 _w_on   _w_it   _w_ant   _w_as   _w_edge

14 _b_lank   _b_loom   _b_lock   _b_lush   _b_owl

15 _g_ate   _g_loss   _g_rain   _g_rind   _g_utter

5

Change the first word of the third pair in the same way as the other pairs to give a new word.

B 18

Example   bind, hind   bare, hare   but, hut

16 flat, that   flan, than   fling, thing

17 tiny, shiny   tatter, shatter   tell, shell

18 spot, tops   loot, tool   pots, stop

19 risk, whisk   rich, which   rose, whose

20 face, fire   space, spire   mace, mire

5

Underline the two words, one from each group, which are closest in meaning.

B 3

Example   (race, shop, <u>start</u>)   (finish, <u>begin</u>, end)

21 (kidnap, take, hold)   (across, abduct, grab)

22 (fat, oil, butter)   (greasy, rich, lubricate)

23 (mean, scarce, merge)   (aged, scanty, solve)

24 (fruit, current, sweet)   (contemporary, cold, cherry)

25 (flabbergast, laugh, amusing)   (cry, flap, astound)

5

Underline the one word in the brackets which will go equally well with both the pairs of words outside the brackets.

B 5

Example   rush, attack   cost, fee   (price, hasten, strike, <u>charge</u>, money)

26 shore, beach   freewheel, glide   (ocean, <u>coast</u>, rocks, cycle, sea)

27 animal, pet   pursue, follow   (wolf, <u>dog</u>, cat, cow, rat)

28 digit, number   form, shape   (whole, <u>figure</u>, set, mould, outline)

29 point, score   aim, target   (ambition, <u>goal</u>, match, game, team)

30 twig, bough   subdivision, offshoot   (root, leaflet, <u>branch</u>, learn, stem)

5

Complete the following sentences by selecting the most sensible word from each group of words given in the brackets. Underline the words selected.

Example   The (<u>children</u>, books, foxes) carried the (houses, <u>books</u>, steps) home from the (greengrocer, <u>library</u>, factory).

31 The (boy, man, <u>dog</u>) (<u>barked</u>, shouted, cried) when he was put on a (walk, <u>lead</u>, foot).

32 Quickly, climb up the (dungeon, <u>tower</u>, door) and look at the (step, arrow, <u>view</u>).

33 (Lakes, buildings, <u>forests</u>) contain (flowers, <u>trees</u>, fish) where many types of (<u>animal</u>, mountain, boat) can make their homes.

34 Our class (teacher, <u>computer</u>, form captain) is always being used in project time to find (books, apples, <u>information</u>) from the Internet.

35 The boy walked (<u>hungrily</u>, quickly, badly) so he had time to (<u>play</u>, work, colour) in the (feelings, <u>puddles</u>, smells).

5

Complete the following expressions by filling in the missing word.

Example   Pen is to ink as brush is to <u>paint</u>.

36 Dawn is to morning as _*dusk*_ is to evening.

37 Legs are to run as wings are to _*fly*_ .

38 Grass is to meadow as sand is to _*beach*_ .

39 Day is to seven as month is to _*twelve*_ .

40 Stop is to red as go is to _*green*_ .

5

Underline the pair of words most opposite in meaning.

Example   cup, mug   coffee, milk   <u>hot, cold</u>

41 request, ask   misery, despair   <u>refuse, offer</u>

42 <u>many, few</u>   last, end   ally, helper

43 <u>asleep, awake</u>   plan, scheme   behaviour, conduct

44 <u>ebb, flow</u>   bad, evil   live, exist

45 remedy, cure   <u>health, ailment</u>   escape, getaway

5

Underline the two words which are the odd ones out in the following groups of words.

Example   black   <u>king</u>   purple   green   <u>house</u>

46 <u>pencil</u>   instruction   lesson   teaching   <u>pen</u>

47 persuade   cajole   <u>believe</u>   coax   <u>guess</u>

48 pigsty   <u>horse</u>   <u>trough</u>   kennel   stable

49 bicycle   <u>road</u>   lorry   <u>rail</u>   bus

50 <u>nephew</u>   grandmother   sister   <u>father</u>   daughter

5

Find a word that can be put in front of each of the following words to make new, compound words.

Example	CAST	FALL	WARD	POUR	<u>DOWN</u>
51	DRAW	STAND	HOLD	OUT	*WITH*
52	PIECE	MIND	CLASS	WORK	*Master*
53	CARE	NOON	EFFECT	SHOCK	*After*
54	STAIRS	SET	RIGHT	HILL	*Up*
55	FALL	CAP	DRESS	LIGHT	*Night*

Fill in the crosswords so that all the given words are included. You have been given one letter as a clue in each crossword.

56–57

turkey, uglier, angles, carpet, points, settee

58–59

etched, aspect, advert, praise, choice, storms

Give the two missing numbers in the following sequences.

Example	2	4	6	8	<u>10</u>	<u>12</u>	
60	8	9	11	14	*18*	23	*29*
61	108	*96*	84	72	60	48	*36*
62	74	60	48	*38*	*30*	24	20
63	11	*13*	12	15	*13*	17	14
64	*4*	2	5	4	6	*6*	7

The twins are having a party on 30 December, Gary's party is three days later, but Cathy is having hers a week before the twins.

65 What day is Gary's party on? *2 January*

66 What day is Cathy's party on? *23 December*

67 The twins have to postpone their party for a fortnight. It is now on *13 January*.

If these words were placed in alphabetical order:

douse   double   down   doubt   dough

68 which word would be last? _down_

69 which word would be first? _double_

70 If the words were written backwards, which would be the last in alphabetical order? _doubt_

B 20

3

Find the letter which will complete both pairs of words, ending the first word and starting the second. The same letter must be used for both pairs of words.

B 10

Example   mea (t) able   fi (t) ub

71 tea (_) isk   pur (_) ope   72 pa (_) ork   pillo (_) eather

73 bul (_) arge   bar (_) ush   74 was (_) ear   sli (_) ond

75 crow (_) od   pla (_) oon

5

Find the four-letter word hidden at the end of one word and the beginning of the next word. The order of the letters may not be changed.

B 21

Example   The children had bats and balls.   _sand_

76 He keeps the stamps from envelopes.   _omen_

77 Mistakes can be easily made.   _scan_

78 She grew inky-blue flowers in the garden.   _wink_

79 It's your turn after mine.   _term_

80 He replied angrily, and ran out.   _here_

5

Now go to the Progress Chart to record your score!   Total   80

Paper 4

Look at the first group of three words. The word in the middle has been made from the other two words. Complete the second group of three words in the same way, making a new word in the middle.

B 18

Example   PAIN INTO TOOK   ALSO SOON ONLY

1 KERB   BARK   ASKS   AJAR _Real_ EELS ✓

2 PITY   TYPE   PEAS   BONE _Nest_ STIR ✓

3 TAIL   WAIT   THAW   SOUR _Foul_ LEAF ✓

4 ENDS   DICE   ICED   SOBS _BEDS_ EDGE ✓

5 TINS   BIND   DRAB   WOOD _TOOK_ KILT ✓

5 5

Find the three-letter word which can be added to the letters in capitals to make a new word. The new word will complete each sentence sensibly.

Example   The cat sprang onto the MO   _USE_ ✓

6 They listen when the teacher SKS.   PEA ✓

7 I like HY on my toast.   ONE ✓

8 The WHER was very cold.   THE ✗

9 He enjoyed PING in the sand.   LAY ✓

10 The house was now VAT.   CAN ✓

Underline two words, one from each group, that go together to form a new word. The word in the first group always comes first.

Example   (hand, <u>green</u>, for)   (light, <u>house</u>, sure)

11 (<u>there</u>, which, when)   (was, time, <u>fore</u>)   ✓

12 (far, <u>near</u>, out)   (hold, <u>law</u>, police)   ✓

13 (<u>in</u>, an, it)   (soft, <u>side</u>, right)   ✓

14 (leg, <u>hand</u>, saw)   (<u>some</u>, ankle, kick)   ✓

15 (top, <u>cap</u>, hat)   (tile, <u>able</u>, list)   ✓

Add one letter to the word in capital letters to make a new word. The meaning of the new word is given in the clue.

Example   PLAN   simple   _plain_

16 REVERE   to turn round   Reverse ✓

17 WING   to squeeze   WRING ✓

18 PEAK   to say something   Speak ✓

19 PACE   quietness   Peace ✓

20 SOON   eating utensil   Spoon ✓

Give the missing number in the following sequences.

Example   2 4 6 8 <u>10</u> 12   ✓

21 4   7   11   16   22 ✓

22 35   44   46   55   57   66   68 ✓

23 3   6   7   10 ✓   11   14   15

24 4   12   11   33   32   96   95 ✓

25 80   75   76   71   72   67   68 ✓

Underline the two words which are the odd ones out in the following groups of words.

Example   black   <u>king</u>   purple   green   <u>house</u>

26 <u>call</u>   hail   frost   <u>whisper</u>   snow ✓

27 <u>book</u>   see   view   <u>programme</u>   watch ✓

28 colour   <u>face</u>   tint   <u>leg</u>   hue ✓

29 write   draw   <u>animal</u>   print   <u>house</u> ✓

30 <u>skin</u>   banana   apple   <u>jelly</u>   peach ✓

5 **5**

Fill in the missing letters or numbers. The alphabet has been written out to help you.

A B C D E F G H I J K L M N O P Q R S T U V W X Y Z

Example   AB is to CD as PQ is to RS

31 AE is to BF as LP is to   MQ ✓

32 12 is to 36 as 17 is to   51 ✓

33 81 is to 27 as 93 is to   39 ✗   (54)

34 49 is to 7 as 81 is to   39 ✗   (42)

35 1000 is to 10 as 10,000 is to   100 ✓

3 **5**

If the code for CLOTHES is ▲ □ ■ ▼ ○ ● ◆, what do the following codes stand for?

36 ◆ ■ ■ ▼ ○ ●   SOOTHE ✓

37 ▲ □ ■ ◆ ●   CLOSE ✓

38 □ ■ ◆ ▼   LOST ✓

What are the codes for the following words?

39 THOSE   ▼●○□◇○ ✓

40 HOST   ○□◇▼ ✓

5 **5**

Underline the pair of words most opposite in meaning.

Example   cup, mug   coffee, milk   <u>hot, cold</u>

41 warm, balmy   <u>fire, ice</u>   burn, flame ✓

42 bed, time   snow, ball   <u>freeze, heat</u> ✓

43 dawn, daybreak   <u>night, morning</u>   milk, bottle ✓

44 <u>sea, land</u> ✓   buy, purchase   bathe, paddle

45 snow, cold   sun, shine   <u>toil, rest</u> ✓

5 **5**

15

Underline the one word in the brackets which will go equally well with both the pairs of words outside the brackets.

Example   rush, attack   cost, fee   (pricel, hasten, strike, <u>charge</u>, money)

46 blackout, giddy   faded, unclear   (fast, ill, faint, well, pure)

47 gale, blast   upset, calamity   (strike, luck, blow, feel, wind)

48 attract, please   spell, magic   (charm, mascot, wizard, interest, draw)

49 chief, main   money, wealth   (town, bank, capital, cash, credit)

50 split, shatter   interval, holiday   (vacation, pause, break, splinter, crumble)

5

Rearrange the muddled words in capital letters so that each sentence makes sense.

Example   There are sixty SNODCES <u>SECONDS</u> in a UTMINE. <u>MINUTE</u>

51 A GNILLOR _____ stone gathers no SOMS _____.

52 There are NEVES _____ days in a KEWE _____.

53 Don't UTNOC _____ your SKINECCH _____ before they are hatched.

54 Cardiff is the TPCAIAL _____ of LESAW _____.

55 There are EVNES _____ colours in the WBRAION _____.

5

Solve the problem by working out the letter code. The alphabet has been written out to help you.

A B C D E F G H I J K L M N O P Q R S T U V W X Y Z

Example   If the code for SECOND is written as UGEQPF, what is the code for THIRD?   <u>VJKTF</u>

56 If the code for TIME is ODHZ, what is the code for CLOCK?   _____

57 If the code for SHADOW is HSZWLD, what is the code for SUNLIGHT? _____

58 If the code for PINK is QJOL, what is the code for BLUE?   _____

59 If the code for BASKET is CBTLFU, what does TUVC mean?   _____

60 If the code for STUDY is QRSBW, what does BSQR mean?   _____

5

Fill in the crosswords so that all the given words are included. You have been given one letter as a clue in each crossword.

61–62

potter, nettle, sicken, astute, sprays, static

63–64

opened, hoping, intend, greets, peanut, kettle

If these words were placed in alphabetical order:

65 baby   school-girl   student   grown-up   pensioner

Which word would be first? _____ _____

66 seed   seedling   leaf   bud   flower

Which word would be last? _____

67 pram   pushchair   tricycle   bicycle   car

Which word would be fourth? _____

68 letter   word   sentence   paragraph   book

Which word would be second? _____

69 none   single   triple   quadruple   double

Which word would be third? _____

Read the first two statements and then underline one of the four options below that must be true.

70 'People are animals. Animals are not wood.'

Some animals are kept as pets.

People build with wood.

People are not wood.

A dog is a type of animal.

Find the two letters which will end the first word and start the second word.

Example   rea (<u>c h</u>) air

71 chis   (__ __) dest   72 hand (__ __) ad

73 chan   (__ __) ese   74 met   (__ __) most

75 cent   (__ __) ad

Find and underline the two words which need to change places for each sentence to make sense.

Example   She went to <u>letter</u> the <u>write</u>.

76 Your is where big sister?

77 My need all pencils sharpening.

78 Some made I scones today.

79 I at having my lunch like school.

80 I take my day out each dog.

Now go to the Progress Chart to record your score!   **Total**   80

Paper 5

Find a word that is similar in meaning to the word in capital letters and that rhymes with the second word.

Example   CABLE   tyre   *wire*

1 ENEMY   doe   foe

2 SUCCESSOR   their   heir

3 UNEVEN   enough   rough

4 PEACEFUL   balm   calm

5 CENTRE   fiddle   middle

Complete the following sentences in the best way by choosing one word from each set of brackets.

Example   Tall is to (tree, <u>short</u>, colour) as narrow is to (thin, white, <u>wide</u>).

6 Jug is to (pour, milk, measure) as glass is to (clear, water, window).

7 Leave is to (<u>come</u>, tree, drop) as part is to (<del>join</del>, piece, act).

8 Fish is to (chips, water, <u>scales</u>) as bird is to (burgers, beak, <u>feathers</u>).

9 Yours is to (hers, its, <u>you</u>) as mine is to (coal, <u>me</u>, them).

10 Conventional is to (<u>odd</u>, easy, worried) as abnormal is to (unusual, peculiar, <u>normal</u>).

Underline the one word in the brackets which will go equally well with both the pairs of words outside the brackets.

Example   rush, attack   cost, fee   (price, hasten, strike, <u>charge</u>, money)

11 solid, lump   obstacle, stop   (hard, <u>block</u>, firm, halt, shape)

12 charge, price   meal, food   (feed, <u>cost</u>, fare, do, supper)

13 clip, trim   yield, produce   (crop, cut, scissors, farm, tidy)

14 column, pole   position, assignment   (cancel, job, post, stamp, appointment)

15 brain, head   resent, dislike   (top, hate, <u>mind</u>, care, bother)

Find the two letters which will end the first word and start the second word.

Example   rea (<u>c h</u>) air

16 spa   (r e) mind

17 parc   (e l) der

18 reme   (_ _) eu

19 spo   (o n) ce

20 tab   (l e) mon

ler

spot   spat

otce   atce

Underline the one word which **cannot be made** from the letters of the word in capital letters.

Example   STATIONERY   stone   tyres   ration   <u>nation</u>   noisy

21 DREAD   dear   <u>bad</u>   red   dead   dare

22 SPATTER   reap   treat   sprat   <u>tease</u>   spear

23 CREMATE   mace   cream   tamer   crate   <u>matter</u>

24 CARPENTER   <u>truce</u>   creep   preen   prance   carpet

25 DISTEMPER   strim   <u>stems</u>   temper   demise   pester

Underline two words, one from each group, that go together to form a new word. The word in the first group always comes first.

Example   (hand, <u>green</u>, for)   (light, <u>house</u>, sure)

26 (high, fight, road)   (shout, noise, <u>light</u>)

27 (rung, rang, ring)   (out, let, off)

28 (ticket, <u>fare</u>, bus)   (punch, gone, <u>well</u>)

29 (under, <u>over</u>, next)   (<u>board</u>, cloth, bored)

30 (<u>cross</u>, tick, ring)   (test, right, bow)

Find the four-letter word hidden at the end of one word and the beginning of the next word. The order of the letters may not be changed.

Example   The children had bats and balls   _sand_

31 We tried to urge our team to win.   ~~tour~~ ✓

32 Out of breath, the last rower lent over his oar.   ~~soar~~ ✓

33 'Which information is correct?' queried the teacher.   ~~clin~~ ✓

34 When you are seated, please attach the safety belt.   ~~seat~~ ✓

35 For old people, climbing steps can be difficult.   ~~Scan~~ ✓

 5

Remove one letter from the word in capital letters to leave a new word. The meaning of the new word is given in the clue.

Example   AUNT   an insect   _ant_

36 SLUSH   abundant   LUSH ✓

37 LAIRD   a den   LAIR ✓

38 MINDED   dug out of the ground   MINED ✓

39 SPRINT   a kind of writing   PRINT

40 BRIDGE   a woman on her wedding day   BRIDE ✓

 5

Complete the following sentences by selecting the most sensible word from each group of words given in the brackets. Underline the words selected.

Example   The (<u>children</u>, books, foxes) carried the (houses, <u>books</u>, steps) home from the (greengrocer, <u>library</u>, factory).

41 The (<u>car</u>, train, plane) which was travelling in the fast (runway, <u>lane</u>, road) ✓ swerved and hit a (pilot, wheel, <u>pedestrian</u>).

42 Please take your (<u>books</u>, marbles, sandwiches) off the teacher's (car, <u>desk</u>, fridge) as you will need them for the next (door, <u>lesson</u>, breakfast). ✓

43 '(Sweets, <u>pink</u>, flowers) is my favourite (chocolate, vase, <u>colour</u>)', she said kindly, ✓ unwrapping the home-made (<u>scarf</u>, puppy, plant).

44 The police arrived quickly at the (site, ground, <u>scene</u>) of the accident, as they ✓ were only a few (years, <u>streets</u>, towns) away.

45 Under cover of (blankets, <u>darkness</u>, trees) the (lioness, baby, <u>thief</u>) climbed ✓ through the warehouse (jungle, <u>window</u>, bed).

 5

20

Fill in the missing letters. The alphabet has been written out to help you.

A B C D E F G H I J K L M N O P Q R S T U V W X Y Z

Example AB is to CD as PQ is to RS ✓

46 AE is to CG as IM is to KO ✓

47 AZB is to BYC as CXD is to DWE ✓

48 EJG is to GLA as INJ is to KPD ✓

49 BDB is to DFD as FHF is to HJH ✓

50 RH is to PJ as ND is to LF ✓

Change the first word into the last word, by changing one letter at a time and making two new, different words in the middle.

Example TEAK TEAT TENT RENT

51 DEAR BEAR BEAT BEST ✓

52 BEND BAND BANK BUNK ✓

53 FALL BALL BELL BELT ✓

54 POTS PATS PASS PAST ✓

55 HULK HULL HALL HALE ✓

Fill in the crosswords so that all the given words are included. You have been given one letter as a clue in each crossword.

56–57

ham, men, den, ore,
are, hod

58–59

hoe, ash, leo, ale,
ewe, sew

Give the two missing numbers in the following sequences.

Example 2 4 6 8 10 12

60 12 15 21 30 42 57 75 ✓

61 7 8 9 16 11 24 13 ✓

62 100 93 86 79 72 65 58 ✓

Change one word so that the sentence makes sense. Underline the word you are taking out and write your new word on the line.

B 14

Example I waited in line to buy a <u>book</u> to see the film. <u>ticket</u>

63 Mia's bike had a flat <u>saddle</u>. tyre ✓

64 As the sun set in the <u>east</u>, Ali watched the shadows lengthen. WEST ✓

65 The high <u>grass</u> that surrounded the castle was designed to keep out the enemy. WALL ✓

66 I find it difficult to thread my <u>cushion</u> in my sewing lessons. NEEDLE ✓

67 Take a tissue and blow your trumpet rather than sniff. ● _____

4 5

If the code for APPEARANCE is @ = = X @ £ @ + ÷ X, what do the following codes stand for?

B 24

68 ÷ @ = X <u>CARE</u> ✓✓

69 @ £ X <u>ARE</u> ✓

What are the codes for the following words?

70 PREEN = £ XX + ✓

71 NEAR + X @ £ ✓

72 PRANCE = £ @ + ÷ X ✓

5 5

Rearrange the letters in capitals to make another word. The new word has something to do with the first two words.

B 16

Example spot soil SAINT <u>STAIN</u>

73 law regulation LURE <u>RULE</u> ✓

74 bandage gauze STAPLER <u>PLASTER</u> ✓ $\frac{7}{2}$

75 cheer gladden ASLEEP <u>PLEASE</u> ✓

76 believe depend STRUT <u>TRUST</u> ✓

77 sea water CANOE <u>OCEAN</u> ✓

5 5

If A = 2, B = 3, C = 4, D = 5, E = 6, F = 7, L = 8, N = 9 find the sum of the following words:

B 26

78 F + A + D + E + D = <u>25</u> ✓

79 C + L + E + A + N = <u>29</u> ✓

80 B + E + A + D = <u>16</u> ✓

3 3

Now go to the Progress Chart to record your score! Total **74 80**

Paper 6

If E = 5, I = 6, P = 8, N = 4, S = 10, R = 12, T = 20, find the sum of the following words:

1 T + E + N = 29 ✓

2 S + E + E + N = 24 ✓

3 P + E + N = 17 ✓

4 P + E + T = 33 ✓

5 T + R + I + P = 46 ✓

Rearrange the letters in capitals to make another word. The new word has something to do with the first two words.

	Example	spot	soil	SAINT	STAIN
6	wrong	incorrect		FLEAS	FALSE ✓
7	close	touching		EARN	NEAR ✓
8	copy	draw		CRATE	TRACE ✓
9	broom	mop		SHRUB	BRUSH ✓
10	diagram	chart		BLEAT	TABLE ✓
11	saying	expression		SERAPH	PHRASE ✓

Write the four-letter word hidden at the end of one word and the beginning of the next word. The order of these letters may not be changed.

Example The children had bats and balls   _sand_

12 They were all caught in a rainstorm.   _real_ ✓

13 He hoped that something would turn up.   _hats_ ✓

14 The youngest toddler cried for his mother.   _they_ ✓

15 Luckily their delays were not too lengthy.   _tool_ ✓

16 I want to run in the race for the charity.   _fort_ ✓

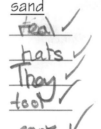

Complete the following sentences by selecting the most sensible word from each group of words given in the brackets. Underline the words selected.

Example The (children, books, foxes) carried the (houses, books, steps) home from the (greengrocer, library, factory). ✓

17 The (TV, trellis, terrace) was covered with (rhubarb, rubbish, roses) which needed (planting, pointing, pruning).

18 The (weather, book, cardigan) was so (exciting, uninteresting, chilly) she did not want to put it down.

(23)

19 The hailstones (drummed, whistled, smoked) on the (chimney, car roof, carpet) as they were driving to (winter, school, distraction).

20 The (savage, docile, tender) dog bit the (fireman, electrician, postman) as he was delivering the (milk, letters, pigeons).

21 He would have to choose the right time of (night, year, day) to (wrestle, water, whistle) the (pillars, plants, penguins).

Find the two letters which will end the first word and start the second word.

Example   rea (c h) air

22 purp   (l e) ague

23 bran   (c h) arge

24 peri   (s h) ield

25 mosa   (i c) icle

26 fast   (e n) gine

Give the next group of letters or numbers in the following sequences. The alphabet has been written out to help you.

A B C D E F G H I J K L M N O P Q R S T U V W X Y Z

27 AE   BF   CG   DH   EI

28 ZK   YL   XM   WN   VO

29 342   453   564   675   786

30 924   835   746   657   568

31 7   15   9   17   11   18 19

Underline the pair of words most similar in meaning.

Example   come, go   roam, wander   fear, fare

32 remember, forget   rest, work   rival, opponent

33 rise, fall   spine, backbone   half, whole

34 recoup, revolve   sure, certain   straight, crooked

35 bluff, pretend   before, after   believe, distrust

36 noise, silence   fair, dark   brave, fearless

Underline the two words in each line which are made from the same letters.

Example   TAP / PET   TEA   POT   EAT

37   TEST   NEST   WENT   TENS   TENT

38   STEP   STAY   TAME   MAZE   PEST

39   PEEP   LEAP   PALE   SLAP   PLAY

40   WEST   REST   STIR   WIRE   STEW

41   LEER   LAIR   REAL   RAIL   RULE

Find and underline the two words which need to change places for each sentence to make sense.

Example   She went to letter the write.

42   There in a lovely smell was the kitchen.

43   I was three was my sister when born.

44   He brave a very was man.

45   She into the flour sieved a bowl.

46   We start soon will school.

The word TEACHER is written in code as ◗ ~ ○ ● ▮ ~ ■
Decode these words.

47   ● ▮ ~ ○ ◗   CHEAT

48   ○ ● ▮ ~   ACHE

49   ◗ ■ ○ ● ~   TRACE

Write these words in code.

50   CRATE   ● ▮ ○ ◗ ~

51   ARCH   ○ ◗ ■ ● ▮

Mouse

Find the three-letter word which can be added to the letters in capitals to make a new word. The new word will complete the sentence sensibly.

Example   The cat sprang onto the MO.   USE

52   They SED at the amazing sight.   TAR

53   He HD the cry of the owl.   EAR   Heard

54   He stuck his GUE out at the boy.   TON   TON   tongue

55   The lion RED.   OAR

56   It was an AE angle.   CUT

25

Underline two words, one from each group, that go together to form a new word.
The word in the first group always comes first.

Example   (hand, <u>green</u>, for)   light, <u>house</u>, sure)

57 (glass, <u>cup</u>, food)   (shelf, floor, <u>board</u>)   *cupboard*

58 (check, tick, <u>cross</u>)   (down, side, <u>word</u>)

59 (by, side, <u>fore</u>)   (<u>ground</u>, paper, wall)

60 (live, healthy, <u>dead</u>)   (key, well, <u>lock</u>)

61 (flood, for, <u>furniture</u>)   (<u>give</u>, away, breakage)

Complete the following expressions by underlining the missing word.

Example   Frog is to tadpole as swan is (duckling, baby, <u>cygnet</u>).

62 Dirty is to soiled as stained is to (sparse, <u>tarnished</u>, several).

63 Loud is to noisy as rowdy is to (strides, walk, <u>boisterous</u>).

64 Chatter is to babble as talk is to (silent, <u>speak</u>, moment).

65 Hungry is to peckish as famished is to (drowning, seeing, <u>starving</u>).

66 Medium is to moderate as middle is to (<u>midway</u>, midday, midland).

Anne and Emma learn ballroom dancing and judo.
Emma and Lucy learn judo and fencing.
Caroline and Anne learn tap dancing and ballroom dancing.

67 Who learns judo but not fencing?   Anne and

68 Who learns ballroom dancing but not tap dancing?   Emma

69 Which activity doesn't Anne learn?   fencing

70 Which activity doesn't Emma learn?   tap dancing

71 How many girls do three activities?   2

Change the first word into the last word, by changing one letter at a time and making two new, different words in the middle.

Example   TEAK   <u>TEAT</u>   <u>TENT</u>   RENT

72 TAKE   LAKE   LIKE   LIVE

73 PIPE   PILL   PILE   HILL

74 GOOD   WOOD   WORD   WORK

75 HOME   HOPE   ROPE   RIPE

76 WARM   WARF   MART   MAST

A B C D E F G H I J K L M N O P Q R S T U V W X Y Z

Spell the following words backwards. Write numbers underneath the words to indicate their new alphabetical order.

B 20

77 FATTEN — 4   LIGHTEN — 2   MOISTEN — 3   SOFTEN — 1

78 COMICAL — 1   FINAL — 4   MUSICAL — 2   OFFICIAL — 3

79 CATCHMENT — 3   FITMENT — 4   ODDMENT — 1   SEGMENT — 2

80 DANCING — 1   CRYING — 4   FLYING — 3   SAYING — 2

4

Now go to the Progress Chart to record your score!   Total   47 / 80

(do above)

Paper 7

Underline the two words which are made from the same letters.

B 7

Example   TAP   PET   <u>TEA</u>   POT   <u>EAT</u>

1   NEED   <u>SEND</u>   MEND   DINS   <u>DENS</u>   PRICE

2   STEM   LOTS   <u>LAST</u>   MIND   MAST   <u>SALT</u>

3   <u>LAPSE</u>   LIMPS   LAMPS   LUMPS   <u>SEPAL</u>   PULSE

4   SPACE   <u>ADDER</u>   STING   <u>DREAD</u>   START   TINTS

5   <u>POST</u>   PORT   POND   PEST   PACK   <u>STOP</u>

5

Move one letter from the first word and add it to the second word to make two new words.

B 13

Example   hunt   sip   <u>hut</u>   <u>snip</u>

6   trust   rend   rust   trend

7   prose   lace   rose   place

8   front   ice   font   rice

9   clean   plan   clan   plane

10   beat   end   eat   bend

5

Complete the following sentences in the best way by choosing one word from each set of brackets.

B 15

Example   Tall is to (tree, <u>short</u>, colour) as narrow is to (thin, white, <u>wide</u>).

11 Pull is to (row, push, run) as out is to (door, down, in).

12 Lean is to (tilt, bumpy, hungry) as flat is to (level, uneven, tall).

13 Chicken is to (grain, coop, egg) as grass is to (seed, green, hay).

14 Adore is to (cherish, dislike, ignore) as doubt is to (question, remember, answer).

15 Ruin is to (build, help, destroy) as find is to (buy, borrow, discover).

5

These number codes match three of the four words given, but you are not told which code matches which word.

B 24

3844   6851   3824   6844
BALL   WAIL   BASE   WALL

Write the correct code next to each word.

16 BALL   6844

17 WAIL   3824

18 BASE   6851

19 WALL   3844

Decode this number:

20 4835   LAWS

5

Underline the word in the brackets closest in meaning to the word in capitals.

B 5

Example   UNHAPPY   (unkind death laughter <u>sad</u> friendly)

21 HAMMER   (shout   call   <u>mallet</u>   strike   hurt)

22 ELASTIC   (ribbon   <u>flexible</u>   hard   clothes   wider)

23 HUNGRY   (tired   listless   thirsty   <u>ravenous</u>   bad)

24 WHOLE   (<u>entire</u>   part   section   sector   big)

25 WASH   (wait   soap   <u>cleanse</u>   towel   brush)

5

Change one word so that the sentence makes sense. Underline the word you are taking out and write your new word on the line.

B 14

Example   I waited in line to buy a <u>book</u> to see the film.   <u>ticket</u>

26 'Happy thirteenth <u>holidays</u>, Warren', shouted his mother.   birthday

27 The <u>cat</u> took her bone to her kennel and quietly ate it.   dog

28 The <u>soldier</u> waved at her subjects as she stood on the balcony at Buckingham Palace.   queen

29 Jamil carefully took down a heavy reference <u>picture</u> from the library shelf and started to read.   book

30 Our <u>newts</u> grew legs and turned into frogs.   tadpoles

5

Find the three-letter word which can be added to the letters in capitals to make a new word. The new word will complete the sentence sensibly.

Example The cat sprang onto the MO. _USE_ ✓

31 He put the SLE on the horse. ADD ✓

32 Where do they SD for the ceremony? TAN ✓

33 Mum likes CUSD on her fruit. TAR ✓

34 The cook put CURTS in the cake. RAN ✓

35 TE are her books. HER ✓

⑤ 5

Give the two missing numbers in the following sequences.

Example 2   4   6   8   _10_   _12_

36 77   70   _63_ ✓   56   49   _42_ ✓

37 38   41   45   _50_ ✓   _56_   63

38 2   _4_ ✓   8   16   _32_ ✓   64

39 5   16   10   14   15   12   _20_ ✓   _10_ ✓

40 80 (-47)   33 (+57)   90 (-51)   39   _100_ ✓   _45_ ✓   110   51

⑤ 5

Find the two letters which will end the first word and start the second word.

Example tea (_c h_) est

41 almo (_s t_) ance

42 tren (_c h_) arge

43 broa (_c h_) eap

44 cri (_e d_) ge

45 ash (_e n_) joy

⑤ 5

Solve the problem by working out the letter code. The alphabet has been written out to help you.

A B C D E F G H I J K L M N O P Q R S T U V W X Y Z

Example If the code for SECOND is UGEQPF, what is the code for THIRD? _VJKTF_

46 If the code for FLEET is 17336, what is the code for LEFT? 7316 ✓

47 If the code for PILLOW is QHMKPV, what is the code for BLANKET? CKBMLDU

48 If the code for HARD is JCTF, what is the code for SOFT? UQHV

49 If the code for BLACK is AKZBJ, what does ROKZRG mean? QNJYQF.

50 If the code for HANDY is JCPFA, what is the code for LUMP? NWOR ✓

⑤ 5

4

Underline one word in the brackets which is most opposite in meaning to the word in capitals.

B 6

Example	WIDE	(broad	vague	long	<u>narrow</u>	motorway)
51	TUTOR	(trainer	instructor	teacher	<u>pupil</u> ✓	master)
52	END	(finish	<u>commence</u>	completion	conclusion	last)
53	TIE	(<u>loosen</u> ✓	unite	fasten	join	clasp)
54	CLIMB	(ascend	rise	increase	<u>descend</u>	grow)
55	SHOW	(exhibition	reveal	<u>hide</u>	count	display)

5

Find a word that can be put in front of each of the following words to make new, compound words.

B 11

Example	CAST	FALL	WARD	POUR	<u>DOWN</u>
56	WEIGHT	BACK	WORK	CLIP	PAPER ✓
57	PANE	SIGN	ACT	PART	COUNTER ✓
58	TAKE	STAND	WEAR	WATER	UNDER ✓
59	GEAR	LAMP	PHONES	LINE	HEAD ✓
60	WEED	SIDE	FRONT	FOOD	SEA ✓

5

Fill in the crosswords so that all the given words are included. You have been given one letter as a clue in each crossword.

B 19

61–62

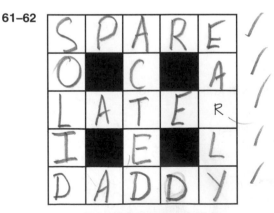

early, solid, spare, daddy,
later, acted

63–64

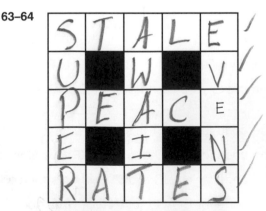

evens, await, super, stale,
rates, peace

65–66

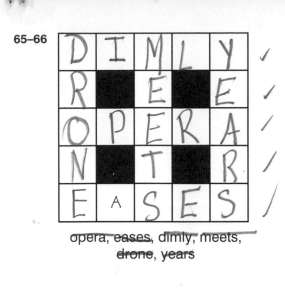

opera, ~~eases~~, ~~dimly~~, ~~meets~~,
~~drone~~, years

~~FURROW~~   ~~FUSE~~   ~~FURNITURE~~   ~~FUSS~~   ~~FURNACE~~

If these words were put in alphabetical order which one would come:

67 first _FURNACE_   **68** last _FUSS_

69 in the middle _FURROW_   **70** fourth _FUSE_

71 second _FURNITURE_

At a riding stables, five stables were empty and five had horses in them. The empty stables are shaded in this diagram.

willow
B–H
T–E

A	B	C	D	E

Willow

F	G	H	I	J

The five horses were:

Beauty   Trigger   Willow   Emily   Halo

Beauty was in the stable next to Halo. Trigger was next to Emily. Trigger was opposite Beauty. Halo was not on the same side as Willow.

Use this information to say which horse was in these stables:

72 A _Emily_   **73** B _Trigger_   **74** E _Willow_

75 G _Beauty_   **76** H _Halo_

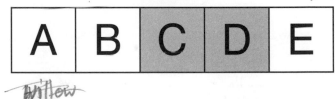

Find and underline the two words which need to change places for each sentence to make sense.

B 17

Example   She went to <u>letter</u> the <u>write</u>.

77   Is Tuesday <u>it</u> or Wednesday <u>tomorrow</u>?

78   Please may I <u>room</u> the <u>leave</u>?

79   Twenty-four <u>four</u> six times <u>is</u>.

80   <u>Fur</u> is as soft as cat's <u>silk</u>.

3   4

Now go to the Progress Chart to record your score!   Total   73   80

Paper 8

Underline the two words, one from each group, which are closest in meaning.

B 3

Example   (race, shop, <u>start</u>)   (finish, <u>begin</u>, end)

1   (water, pit, <u>trap</u>)   (door, fall, <u>snare</u>)

2   (borrow, <u>let</u>, rent)   (flat, <u>allow</u>, own)

3   (<u>too</u>, pear, seventh)   (<u>also</u>, two, heaven)

4   (<u>bowl</u>, field, town)   (bat, <u>dish</u>, country)

5   (watch, <u>observe</u>, sea)   (time, <u>survey</u>, shore)

4   5

Find and underline the two words which need to change places for each sentence to make sense.

B 17

Example   She went to <u>letter</u> the <u>write</u>.

6   Is <u>too</u> bath <u>your</u> hot?

7   I <u>may</u> it <u>think</u> snow today.

8   Did <u>at</u> leave it <u>you</u> the club?

9   I've <u>her</u> to meet <u>got</u> at 1 o'clock.

10   I put <u>on</u> book <u>the</u> the shelf.

5   5

If the code for SURGEON is 4783652, what are the codes for the following words?

B 24

11   SOON <u>4552</u>   12   GONE <u>3526</u>

13   ROSE <u>8546</u>   14   OURS <u>5784</u>

What does this code stand for?

15   27846 <u>NURSE</u>

5   5

Look at the first group of three words. The word in the middle has been made from the other two words. Complete the second group of three words in the same way, making a new word in the middle of the group.

Example   PAIN INTO TOOK   ALSO SOON ONLY

16 DEAR READ ARID   HEAP PEAK DISK
17 HAVE ACHE ICON   AMEN MOAN SOUR
18 STUB BEST DAZE   ALES SEAL TIME
19 PANT TAKE BIKE   LOOP PORT CART
20 LUCK CULT COLT   RUSK TURN TEEN

Fill in the crosswords so that all the given words are included. You have been given one letter as a clue in each crossword.

21–22

tunnel, letter, player, futile, insist, tidily

23–24

dancer, shamed, grated, direct, banish, scream

25–26

sprays, remote, asters, parole, spread, adders

25 / 26 so far...

five fluffy furry awful females fought in fifteen forests after the performance.

33

Find the two letters which will end the first word and start the second word.

Example   rea (<u>c</u> h) air

27 cra   (t e)   nth ✓

28 tow   (e l)   bow ✓

29 gra   (i n)   sect ✓

30 tab   (l e)   aves ✓

31 mot   (o r)   gan ✓

⑤ 5

Find the four-letter word hidden at the end of one word and the beginning of the next word. The order of the letters may not be changed.

Example   The children had bats and balls   <u>sand</u>

32 He baited the hook and tested the rod.   hero ✓

33 It never entered my head.   rent ✓

34 I remember when he was head teacher.   wash ✓

35 Few things, however, have shaken him.   show ✓

36 He broke the school record for the long jump.   fort ✓

⑤ 5

37–40 Look at these groups of words.

A	B	C	D
travel documents	land types	weather	materials

Choose the correct group for each of the words below. Write in the letter.

rainforest B   passport A   tempest C   cotton D   gale C   tickets A

visa A   grassland B   silk D   mountains B   tornado C   wool D

④ 4

Rearrange the letters in capitals to make another word. The new word has something to do with the first two words.

Example   spot   soil   SAINT   STAIN

41 widen   enlarge   KITCHEN   THICKEN ✓

42 bound   fastened   DIET   TIED ✓

43 prize   honour   DRAWER   REWARD ✓

44 threaded   hung   GRUNTS   STRUNG ✓

45 answer   decode   LOVES   SOLVE ✓

⑤ 5

Find a word that can be put in front of each of the following words to make a new, compound word.

	Example	CAST	FALL	WORD	POUR	DOWN
46	STORM	BOLT		CLOUD	CLAP	THUNDER ✓
47	MASTER	LIGHT		DRESS	QUARTERS	HEAD ✓
48	PASTE	ACHE		BRUSH	PICK	TOOTH ✓
49	WRITING	KERCHIEF		SHAKE	CUFF	HAND ✓
50	NAIL	TIP		PRINT	MARK	FINGER ✓

⑤ 5

Give the two missing numbers in the following sequences.

	Example	2	4	6	8	10	12
51	17	25	33	41	49	57	✓
52	59	55	51	47	43	39	✓
53	5	10	20	40	80	160	✓
54	3	11	6	21	9	31	12	41 ✓

55 24 ÷12 36 —6 30 –3 27 +9 36 ×–18 18   15   36 •
    8   12   10   9   12   6   5   12

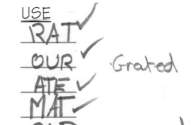

④ 5

Find the three-letter word which can be added to the letters in capitals to make a new word. The new word will complete the sentence sensibly.

Example   The cat sprang onto the MO.   USE ✓

56 The cook GED the cheese.   RAT ✓

57 He wanted to play golf on the new CSE.   OUR ✓   Grated

58 She bathed the cut with cold WR.   ATE ✓

59 The team was beaten in the CH.   MAT ✓

60 Her hair was a lovely GEN colour.   OLD ✓

25
38
⑤ 5

A, B and C went out for a meal. A and B had sausages and C had fish.
A and C had chips and B had mashed potatoes.
A had ice cream.
B and C had trifle.
B and C had coffee.

63 so far...

61 Who had fish, chips and trifle?

62 Who had sausages, chips and ice cream?

63 Who had sausages, mashed potato and trifle?

64 Who had trifle and coffee?

65 Who had coffee but no chips?

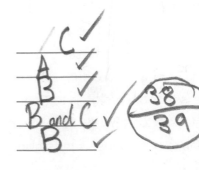

C ✓
A ✓
B ✓
B and C ✓   38/39 so far...
B ✓
⑤ 5

35

Complete the following sentences by selecting the most sensible word from each group of words given in the brackets. Underline the words selected.

B 14

Example The (<u>children</u>, books, foxes) carried the (houses, <u>books</u>, steps) home from the (greengrocer, <u>library</u>, factory).

66 It was the Romans who (sailed, built, paid) a city on the north (bank, bunk, back) of the Thames.

67 The Romans (bought, constructed, enjoyed) a huge (wall, ladder, slope) around the town and they also built (discos, studios, markets).

68 At the end of the (road, film, cinema) the girls left crying because the (story, seats, cars) had been so (boring, sad, hard).

69 As night began to (fall, land, sea), the shadows (watched, lengthened, tightened) and the sun (sat, set, rose).

4

Choose two words, one from each set of brackets, to complete the sentences in the best way.

B 15

Example Smile is to happiness as (drink, <u>tear</u>, shout) is to (whisper, laugh, <u>sorrow</u>).

70 Foot is to toe as (elbow, leg, hand) is to (finger, thumb, glove).

71 One is to single as (four, two, set) is to (add, double, twins).

72 Skin is to man as (tail, claw, hide) is to (animal, cat, baby).

73 Sad is to sorrow as (please, happy, hate) is to (pleading, joy, outing).

74 Oath is to vow as (pledge, memo, rule) is to (argue, promise, follow).

5

If A = 1, C = 2, E = 3, F = 4, D = 5, T = 6, R = 7, P = 8, find the sum of these words when the letters are added together:

B 26

75 TREAD = ___   76 PEER = ___   77 TREAT = ___

78 REAP = ___   79 FACED = ___   80 TRACED = ___

6

Now go to the Progress Chart to record your score!   **Total**   80

Paper 9

Complete the following expressions by underlining the missing word.

B 15

Example Frog is to tadpole as swan is to (duckling, baby, <u>cygnet</u>).

1 House is to brick as nest is to (egg, stick, bird).

2 Full is to empty as cloudy is to (windy, water, clear).

3 Saw is to tooth as toe is to (foot, nail, sock).

4 Confess is to admit as lie is to (acknowledge, deceive, accept).

5 Calf is to bull as foal is to (stallion, horse, mare).

5

Find the four-letter word which can be added to the letters in capitals to make a new word. The new word will complete the sentence sensibly.

Example   They enjoyed the BCAST.   ROAD

6   I am so hot and thirsty I feel PED.   _____

7   Brazil is in the southern HEMISP   _____

8   They chose SAL of the items because one was not enough.   _____

9   The PER has come off the cut on my finger.   _____

10   The blocked DS overflowed.   _____

Find two letters which will end the first word and start the second word.

Example   rea (c h) air

11   bru   (__ __)   ove

12   cat   (__ __)   ew

13   ha   (__ __)   ve

14   radi   (__ __)   ine

15   brid   (__ __)   ader

Rearrange the muddled letters in capitals to make a proper word. The answer will complete the sentence sensibly.

Example   A BEZAR is an animal with stripes.   ZEBRA

16   OISPDLHN are aquatic mammals.   _____

17   You will find the SMDIYRAP in Egypt.   _____

18   Rabbits RRPCDOEUE at an alarming rate.   _____

19   HHCTATDE roofs are made of reeds or straw.   _____

20   In an MGRNYEECE dial 999.   _____

Underline two words, one from each group, that go together to form a new word. The word in the first group always comes first.

Example   (hard, green, for)   (light, house, sure)

21   (birth, life, cradle)   (less, more, much)

22   (pick, slow, set)   (end, back, forward)

23   (smoke, pipe, match)   (wire, water, line)

24   (out, inside, walk)   (warm, rage, temper)

25   (before, after, soon)   (theatre, bed, wards)

Change the first word of the third pair in the same way as the other pairs to give a new word.

B 18

Example   bind, hind   bare, hare   but, <u>hut</u>

26 why, while   sty, stile   my, _____

27 pole, slop   nape, span   rite, _____

28 faster, fight   master, might   plaster, _____

29 mother, moth   tinsel, tins   spares, _____

30 flame, male   blast, salt   write, _____

5

Move one letter from the first word and add it to the second word to make two new words.

B 13

Example   hunt   sip   <u>hut</u>   <u>snip</u>

31 bear   link   _____   _____

32 clean   breath   _____   _____

33 land   fake   _____   _____

34 done   well   _____   _____

35 splice side   _____   _____

5

Find and underline the two words which need to change places for each sentence to make sense.

B 17

Example   She went to <u>letter</u> the <u>write</u>.

36 I'm some I've made sure mistakes.

37 There are the bargains in some sale.

38 I for take my dog must a walk.

39 What is the boy of that name?

40 I soon go to bed must.

5

Underline the word in the brackets which goes best with the words given outside the brackets.

B 1

Example   word, paragraph, sentence   (pen, cap, <u>letter</u>, top, stop)

41 mend, renew   (break, damage, restore, injure)

42 part, section   (whole, portion, none, full)

43 rein, check   (curb, bridle, saddle, loose)

44 misleading, confusing (revolved, puzzling, complain, reflex)

45 dislodge, displace   (rehouse, eject, disorder, dismay)

5

Give the two missing pairs of letters in the following sequences. The alphabet has been written out to help you.

B 23

A B C D E F G H I J K L M N O P Q R S T U V W X Y Z

Example	CQ	DQ	EP	FP	*GO*	*HO*
46 BB	___	DH	___	FN	GQ	
47 ___	UF	XC	SH	VE	___	
48 FS	IQ	HO	___	JK	___	
49 ___	___	JK	NO	RS	VW	
50 QR	___	YN	___	GJ	KH	
51 OR	SV	WZ	___	___	IL	

○ 6

Give the missing number in the following sequences.

B 23

Example	2	4	6	8	*10*	12
52 3	10	15	22	27	___	39
53 5	3	12	10	___	17	26
54 46	55	64	73	___	91	100
55 8	___	22	29	36	43	50
56 234	___	256	267	278	289	300

○ 5

57 Write the letters of the word OSTRICH in the order in which they appear in the dictionary.

B 20

_____

58 If the letters in the following word are arranged in alphabetical order, which letter comes in the middle?

EXTRAVAGANT

_____

59 Write the following words in alphabetical order.

CLEAN   CLAP   CLASP   CLING   CLOSE

_____   _____   _____   _____   _____

○ 3

If the code for FACILE is 6H7C4X, what do the following codes stand for?

B 24

60 6H7X _____   61 74C66 _____

If the code for PASTRY is 4XY6AT, what are the codes for the following words?

62 PART _____   63 TASTY _____   64 START _____

If the code for LOWER is X43YZ, what do the following codes stand for?

65 Z43YZ _____   66 344X _____

○ 7

Read the first two statements and then underline two of the options below that must be true.

67–68 'My car is red, so are fire engines. My sister's car is a Ford, Ford make vans.'

All Ford cars are red.	I like Ford cars.
My car is a Ford.	Ford make fire engines.
I have a fire engine.	Ford make cars.
My sister's car is red.	Fire engines have a siren.
Fire engines are red.	My sister is a fire fighter.

Read the first three statements and then underline two of the options below that must be true.

69–70 'Wasps are insects. Insects do not have internal skeletons. Many insects can fly.'

Wasps have a nasty sting.	All insects are wasps.
Wasps have yellow and black stripes.	Insects have 3 parts to their bodies.
All wasps do not have bones.	Wasps like rotting fruit.
You do not need bones to fly.	All insects fly.
Angry wasps should be avoided.	

4

If a = 10, b = 8, c = 6, d = 5, e = 4, f = 3 find the value of:

B 26

71 (c + d + e) ÷ a = ___

72 cd ÷ a = ___

73 (ef ÷ c) + b = ___

74 $\dfrac{4a}{2d}$ = ___

75 $\dfrac{2ab}{2de}$ = ___

5

Underline the two words which are the odd ones out in the following groups of words.

B 4

Example	black	king	purple	green	house
76 guitar	music	piano	drums	volume	
77 scarce	infrequent	sufficient	adequate	rare	
78 crimson	azure	navy	scarlet	ruby	
79 alike	uniform	outfit	similar	material	
80 smell	speak	ear	sneeze	eye	

5

Now go to the Progress Chart to record your score!   Total   80

Paper 10

Underline the two words which are made from the same letters.

Example	TAP	PET	<u>TEA</u>	POT	<u>EAT</u>
1 ALTER	ALTAR	TALLER	LATER	BLEAT	RATTER
2 CRUSH	SHRUB	CRASH	BLURB	BRUISE	BRUSH
3 BRAKE	STRIKE	CRATE	TRACE	TRACK	STACK
4 STRANGE	STAGE	LABEL	STABLE	BLEATS	BLOATER
5 TOWELS	LOWEST	SLOWER	WORST	LAWYER	FLOWER

5

Find and underline the two words which need to change places for each sentence to make sense.

Example She went to <u>letter</u> the <u>write</u>.

6 What think do you time she will arrive?

7 I hope her have one of we special lunches.

8 Where new your is coat?

9 Do by think she will come you car?

10 I hope I well play will this afternoon.

5

Underline the pair of words most opposite in meaning.

Example	cup, mug	coffee, milk	<u>hot</u>, <u>cold</u>
11	contradict, agree	tired, weary	cold, shivering
12	disease, sickness	hint, suggestion	guilty, innocent
13	reduce, increase	bad, evil	require, need
14	submit, yield	glut, insufficiency	means, resources
15	milk, water	angry, cross	divide, multiply

5

Read the first two statements and then underline one of the four options below that must be true.

16 'Eating sweets can damage your teeth. Eating sweets can make you ill.'

People who are ill have bad teeth.

People with bad teeth have eaten too many sweets.

Sweets can be damaging to people.

People who are ill have been eating too many sweets.

Read the first two statements and then underline one of the four options below that must be true.

17 'Rabbits and guinea pigs are rodents. Rabbits and guinea pigs make good pets.'

    All rodents live in cages.

    All pets are rodents.

    Some rodents make good pets.

    Rabbits eat carrots.

Read the first two statements and then underline one of the five options below that must be true.

18 'A reservoir is a lake that stores water for people to use. Lake Windermere is in Cumbria.'

    Cumbria is a reservoir.

    Lake Windermere is a reservoir.

    People use Lake Windermere.

    A reservoir provides water.

    People drink the water from Lake Windermere.

Read the first two statements and then underline one of the four options below that must be true.

19 'Henry VIII had six wives. Elizabeth I was Henry's daughter.'

    Henry's family name was Tudor.

    Henry was Elizabeth's father.

    Elizabeth was a good queen.

    Henry and Elizabeth ruled for many years.

Underline the word in the brackets closest in meaning to the word in capitals.

	Example	UNHAPPY	(unkind	death	laughter	<u>sad</u>	friendly)
20	MIND		(stay	wait	care	fuss	rest)
21	TEPID		(hot	soapy	lukewarm	soft	cool)
22	CHERISH		(hate	treasure	annoy	ignore	reject)
23	COOK		(ingredients	recipe	oven	heat	bake)
24	HALT		(rest	pause	unsure	stop	hesitate)

Give the two missing numbers in the following sequences.

	Example	2	4	6	8	<u>10</u>	<u>12</u>		
25	111	106	101	___	___	86			
26	81	___	63	___	45	36			
27	5	10	14	___	___	20			
28	666	66.6	___	___	0.0666				
29	6	___	12	20	___	24	24	28	

Find the four-letter word hidden at the end of one word and the beginning of the next word. The order of the letters may not be changed.

B 21

Example The children had bats and balls   _sand_

30 The letters often arrived late. _____

31 I love the books in that series. _____

32 That question cannot be answered. _____

33 'This entails a lot of work', moaned the pupil. _____

34 Mrs Brown had four operations on her knee. _____

5

Find a word that can be put in front of each of the following words to make new, compound words.

B 11

Example CAST   FALL   WARD   POUR   _DOWN_

35 BOW   FALL   PROOF   WATER   _____

36 HOUSE   SHIP   HEARTED   WEIGHT   _____

37 DREAM   BREAK   LIGHT   TIME   _____

38 HOLD   OUT   DRAW   IN   _____

39 CURRANT MAIL   BIRD   BOARD   _____

5

If the code for FLOWER is H2G4ZR, what do the following codes stand for?

B 24

40 4Z22 _____   41 H2ZZ _____

Write the code for the following word.

42 ROLE _____

If the code for PICTURE is 24738XZ, what are the codes for the following words?

43 RIPE _____   44 TRIPPER _____

5

If these words were placed in alphabetical order, which word would come 4th?

B 20

45 forgive   field   forfeit   foreign   furrow   _____

46 gymnast   guild   gracious   guard   guinea   _____

47 quintet   quilt   quiet   question   quit   _____

48 interrupt into   internal   interplay   interrogate   _____

49 pedicure   person   peculiar   penalty   pedigree   _____

5

Find the letter which will complete both pairs of words, ending the first word and starting the second. The same letter must be used for both pairs of words.

B 10

Example mea (t̠) able   fi (t̠) ub

50 hal (_) men   pol (_) ffice

51 epi (_) arp   pani (_) oat

52 thin (_) naw   plu (_) oat

53 pon (_) ash   blin (_) eep

54 clas (_) ark   eart (_) it

5

Find the three-letter word which can be added to the letters in capitals to make a new word. The new word will complete the sentence sensibly.

B 22

Example The cat sprang onto the MO.   USE

55 There was a BCH of the bank nearby.   _____

56 He looked different with a BD.   _____

57 I will GLY do it for you.   _____

58 Put your vote in the BOT box.   _____

59 The JNEY was long and tiring.   _____

5

Move one letter from the first word and add it to the second word to make two new words.

B 13

Example hunt   sip   hut   snip

60 place   ride   _____   _____

61 danger   read   _____   _____

62 crease   filly   _____   _____

63 glance   listen   _____   _____

64 bellow   bride   _____   _____

5

Solve the problem by working out the letter code. The alphabet has been written out to help you.

B 24

A B C D E F G H I J K L M N O P Q R S T U V W X Y Z

Example If the code for SECOND is written as UGEQPF, what is the code for THIRD?   VJKTF

65 If the code for JEWEL is OJBJQ, what is the code for DIAMOND?   _____

66 If the code for ALARM is EPEVQ, what is the code for WARN?   _____

67 If the code for BATCH is 93425, what is the code for CHAT?   _____

68 If the code for TINY is WLQB, what does VPDOO mean?   _____

69 If the code for RINSE is SHORF, what is the code for BELLS?   _____

5

Choose two words, one from each set of brackets, to complete the sentences in the best way.

B 15

Example   Smile is to happiness as (drink, <u>tear</u>, shout) is to (whispers, laugh, <u>sorrow</u>).

70   Broad is to wide as (month, move, more) is to (motion, use, modern).

71   Pant is to gasp as (up, overseas, side) is to (down, abroad, little).

72   Win is to lose as (over, soft, gentle) is to (on, under, between).

73   Rude is to polite as (peace, hate, fight) is to (height, war, enemy).

74   Know is to understand as (clear, clean, clever) is to (dirty, land, lucid).

5

Fill in the crosswords so that all the given words are included. You have been given one letter as a clue in each crossword.

B 19

75–76

caring, buying, slight, entail, blight, unfurl

77–78

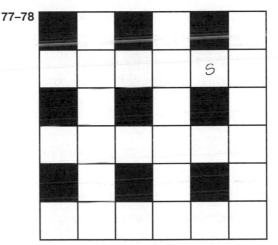

hearse, person, seaman, decide, wigwam, crowns

79–80

valued, caller, target, privet, sleeve, really

6

Paper 11

Read the first two statements and then underline one of the four options below that must be true.

1 'People like living in houses. Houses are usually made of brick.'

  Some people live in flats.

  Houses are popular.

  Houses have gardens.

  All houses are built of brick.

Read the first two statements and then underline one of the four options below that must be true.

2 'Houses have to be heated. Most people have central heating.'

  People don't have coal fires now.

  Houses need some form of heating.

  Everyone has central heating.

  Central heating is better than other forms of heating.

Read the first two statements and then underline one of the four options below that must be true.

3 'Most houses have a garden. Some gardens are neglected.'

  Not all gardens are looked after.

  Some people are keen gardeners.

  Some people are too busy to garden.

  All gardens have flowers.

3

Fill in the crosswords so that all the given words are included. You have been given one letter as a clue in each crossword.

4–5

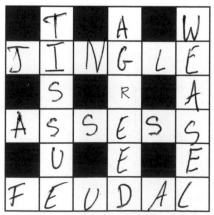

jingle, agreed, feudal, weasel, assess, tissue

6–7

breach, yellow, braise, winced, parcel, shadow

4

Underline the one word in the brackets which will go equally well with both the pairs of words outside the brackets.

    Example   rush, attack   cost, fee   (price, hasten, strike, <u>charge</u>, money)

8 fresh, unheated   poised, controlled   (cold, cool, <u>windy</u>, damp, calm)

9 exact, precise   amend, repair   (tool, dart, <u>correct</u>, fault, fix)

10 beak, nose   charge, account   (bill, bird, man, fee, receipt)

11 sketch, picture   lottery, sweepstake   (paint, pull, <u>draw</u>, ticket, pool)

12 talon, nail   scratch, scrape   (clay, scissors, <u>claw</u>, beak, point)

Underline two words, one from each group, that go together to form a new word. The word in the first group always comes first.

    Example   (hand, <u>green</u>, for)   (light, <u>house</u>, sure)

13 (circus, <u>round</u>, stalls)   (under, <u>about</u>, place)

14 (<u>some</u>, most, many)   (whon, the, <u>how</u>)

15 (bat, <u>just</u>, catch)   (fast, drop, ice)

16 (string, <u>ball</u>, loop)   (net, <u>room</u>, team)

17 (wheel, pedal, <u>spokes</u>)   (<u>air</u>, ring, man)

Find a word that is similar in meaning to the word in capital letters and that rhymes with the second word.

    Example   CABLE   tyre   <u>wire</u>

18 COOP   hen   <u>den</u>

19 PONY   coal   ~~shoat~~ foal

20 MASS   loud   _____

21 IDEA   potion   _____

22 UNITE   coin   <u>join</u>

Find the letter which will complete both pairs of words, ending the first word and starting the second. The same letter must be used for both pairs of words.

    Example   mea (<u>t</u>) able   fi (<u>t</u>) ub

23 grow (<u>l</u>) ad   peta (<u>l</u>) oft

24 ple (<u>a</u>) rc   banan (<u>a</u>) nswer

25 eas (_) arn   tast (_) lm

26 migh (_) eam   toas (_) win

27 tea (_) ind   lar (_) ill

Find and underline the two words which need to change places for each sentence to make sense.

Example   She went to <u>letter</u> the <u>write</u>.

28 When does the next <u>start</u> <u>term</u>?

29 <u>Be</u> must try to <u>I</u> neater.

30 I'd <u>for</u> a bicycle <u>love</u> my birthday.

31 Where <u>paper</u> you put the <u>did</u>?

32 It is <u>living</u> lovely <u>very</u> in the country.

A B C D E F G H I J K L M N O P Q R <u>S</u> T U V W X Y Z

If the code for SECOND is UGEQPF, what are the codes for the following words?

33 SIXTH   UKZVJ

34 FOURTH   HQWTVJ

If the code for STOUT is RSNTS, what are the codes for the following words?

35 FIRST   EHQRS

36 FRONT   EQPMS

37 BIGGER   AHFFDQ

If a = 5, b = 2, c = 0, d = 10, e = 3, find the value of the following calculations.

38 $\dfrac{ac}{b}$ = __

39 bdc = __

40 e + a + c + b = __

41 $d^2 - e^2$ = __

42 (d ÷ a) + e = __

Complete the following expressions by underlining the missing word.

Example   Frog is to tadpole as swan is to (duckling, baby, <u>cygnet</u>).

43 Glitter is to shine as sparkle is to (tinkle, <u>twinkle</u>, wrinkle).

44 Tip over is to knock over as spill is to (<u>upset</u>, sorry, <u>swill</u>).

45 Giggle is to laugh as chuckle is to (flitter, twitter, titter).

46 Huge is to great as vast is to (small, big, <u>immense</u>).

47 Small is to little as tiny is to (large, <u>minute</u>, <u>second</u>).

(48)

Underline one word in the brackets which is most opposite in meaning to the word in capitals.

Example   WIDE   (broad   vague   long   <u>narrow</u>   motorway)

48 COLLECT   (papers   letters   <u>deliver</u>   box   gather)

49 CAUSE   (<u>result</u>   aid   win   lose   reason)

50 MOST   (none   lot   <u>least</u>   multitude   greatest)

51 PARTIAL   (potion   portion   slice   complete   share)

52 PROMPT   (urge   late   quick   immediate   force)

B 6

5

Underline the one word which **cannot be made** from the letters of the word in capital letters.

Example   STATIONERY   stone   tyres   ration   <u>nation</u>   noisy

53 CUSTARD   rust   crust   <u>trace</u>   curd   dust

54 PLEASED   plea   dale   deep   <u>read</u>   seed

55 MANAGER   <u>dear</u>   game   mean   near   ream

56 DEPART   part   trade   <u>tart</u>   trap   dear

57 TEACHER   rate   each   <u>hatchet</u>   chart   hear

B 7

5

Change the first word of the third pair in the same way as the other pairs to give a new word.

Example   bind, hind   bare, hare   but, <u>hut</u>

58 kind, mind   kiss, miss   kink, think

59 page, gape   last, salt   lose, _____

60 cleanest, slowest   clean, slow   cleaning, slowly

61 rent, tore   veal, love   tear, _____

62 blot, bolt   from, form   gaol, goal

B 18

5

Find the four-letter word which can be added to the letters in capitals to make a new word. The new word will complete the sentence sensibly.

Example   They enjoyed the BCAST.   <u>ROAD</u>

63 Carys jumped off the wall and SPED her ankle.   <u>RAIN</u>

64 The postman DERED the letters.   <u>LIVE</u>

65 He enjoys POLIG his shoes.   <u>SHIN</u>

66 Their CLESS chatter was annoying.   _____

67 The film was scary and very SUSEFUL.   _____

shin

B 22

5

49

Move one letter from the first word and add it to the second word to make two new words.

	Example	hunt	sip	_hut_	_snip_
68	train	old	_____	_____
69	beat	gin	_____	_____
70	plant	ten	_____	_____
71	miles	coy	_____	_____
72	crust	old	_____	_____

5

Give the missing number in the following sequences.

	Example	2	4	6	8	_10_	12
73	14	46	78	110	__
74	17	22	29	34	__
75	4	14	22	32	__
76	3	5	8	12	__
77	100	91	83	76	__

5

If the months were put in alphabetical order, which would be:

78 the last month? _____

79 the first month? _____

80 the month after April? _____

3

Now go to the Progress Chart to record your score!   Total   80

Paper 12

Underline the two words, one from each group, which are closest in meaning.

	Example	(race, shop, <u>start</u>)	(finish, <u>begin</u>, end)
1	(individual, looks, charm)	(different, similar, personal)
2	(law, emergency, crime)	(disorder, policeman, offence)
3	(burden, flaw, value)	(thick, worth, loyal)
4	(counter, obtain, expensive)	(acquire, buy, shop)
5	(ordinary, plain, fancy)	(vague, safe, normal)

5

Look at the first group of three words. The word in the middle has been made from the other two words. Complete the second group of three words in the same way, making a new word in the middle of the group.

B 18

Example   PAIN INTO TOOK   ALSO <u>SOON</u> ONLY

6   MIST   TRIM   RARE   TRIP   _____   BEAN

7   BAKE   KEEP   PEST   IRON   _____   ECHO

8   LINT   PILE   PENS   GIRL   _____   SNOW

9   BUST   STUB   BULB   FATE   _____   CALM

10   KEPT   WINK   TWIN   NOTE   _____   FEAR

5

Find the four-letter word which can be added to the letters in capitals to make a new word. The new word will complete the sentence sensibly.

B 22

Example   They enjoyed the BCAST.   <u>ROAD</u>

11   The king wore his magnificent N on special occasions.   _____

12   The bees SED from the hive.   _____

13   Her voice is quite HE from cheering the team on.   _____

14   She went to the SUPERET for the weekly shop.   _____

15   The CE of the river was up in the hills.   _____

5

Find the letter which will complete both pairs of words, ending the first word and starting the second. The same letter must be used for both pairs of words.

R 10

Example   mea (<u>t</u>) able   fi (<u>t</u>) ub

16   puls (__) lder   thre (__) qual

17   cran (__) ing   brea (__) now

18   sta (__) oil   ker (__) ee

19   brai (__) well   po (__) rain

20   tri (__) ain   car (__) lease

5

Which word in each group contains only the first six letters of the alphabet?

B 18

Example   defeat   farce   abide   <u>deaf</u>   dice

21   arrow   bead   beach   creed   bread

22   adder   badge   each   face   dance

23   dread   cadge   deed   ache   decks

24   feeds   daft   fall   coffee   efface

25   card   café   feeble   buff   dabble

5

Underline two words, one from each group, that go together to form a new word. The word in the first group always comes first.

Example   (hand, <u>green</u>, for)   (light, <u>house</u>, sure)

26 (hammer, axe, key)   (wood, tool, hole)

27 (month, nose, frown)   (dive, walk, run)

28 (fish, catch, net)   (duty, work, offer)

29 (soft, loud, noise)   (rumble, quiet, speaker)

30 (out, under, place)   (see, look, watch)

B 8

5

Find the four-letter word hidden at the end of one word and the beginning of the next word. The order of the letters may not be changed.

Example   The children had bats and balls   <u>sand</u>

31 I have information for you.   _____

32 They are staying in a nearby hotel.   _____

33 Be careful! They'll get wind of it soon. _____

34 You must pursue the course.   _____

35 The boy broke his ankle.   _____

B 21

5

Change the first word into the last word, by changing one letter at a time and making two new, different words in the middle.

Example   TEAK   <u>TEAT</u>   <u>TENT</u>   RENT

36 FRAY   _____ _____ TEAM

37 DENT   _____ _____ BAND

38 TRAY   _____ _____ GRIP

39 MOLE   _____ _____ HELD

40 LAKE   _____ _____ FARM

B 13

5

Complete the following sentences by selecting the most sensible word from each group of words given in the brackets. Underline the words selected.

Example   The (<u>children</u>, books, foxes) carried the (houses, <u>books</u>, steps) home from the (greengrocer, <u>library</u>, factory).

41 The (look, book, watch) was about a (duet, jingle, couple) who (cried, travelled, ice-skated) around Australia.

42 Three (cheers, claps, drinks) for the yachtswoman who circumnavigated the (sea, world, sitting room) in her (slippers, rocket, boat).

43 The weatherman said that we can expect (rain, weather, nothing) today with (snow, sand, sea travel) on high (tea, ground, beach).

B 14

44 'Please (give, take, support) generously to the (effect, cause, because)', asked the charity (shop, worker, card).

45 Tessa (painted, dirtied, tidied) her bedroom each (hour, night, week) before she went to (lunch, France, bed).

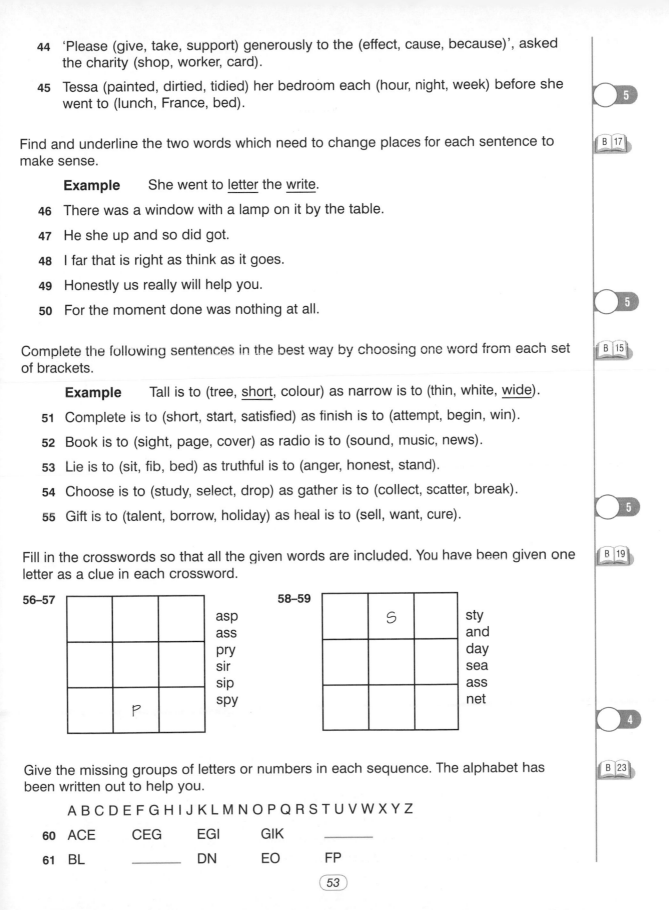

Find and underline the two words which need to change places for each sentence to make sense.

Example She went to <u>letter</u> the <u>write</u>.

46 There was a window with a lamp on it by the table.

47 He she up and so did got.

48 I far that is right as think as it goes.

49 Honestly us really will help you.

50 For the moment done was nothing at all.

Complete the following sentences in the best way by choosing one word from each set of brackets.

Example Tall is to (tree, <u>short</u>, colour) as narrow is to (thin, white, <u>wide</u>).

51 Complete is to (short, start, satisfied) as finish is to (attempt, begin, win).

52 Book is to (sight, page, cover) as radio is to (sound, music, news).

53 Lie is to (sit, fib, bed) as truthful is to (anger, honest, stand).

54 Choose is to (study, select, drop) as gather is to (collect, scatter, break).

55 Gift is to (talent, borrow, holiday) as heal is to (sell, want, cure).

Fill in the crosswords so that all the given words are included. You have been given one letter as a clue in each crossword.

56–57

	P	

asp
ass
pry
sir
sip
spy

58–59

	S	

sty
and
day
sea
ass
net

Give the missing groups of letters or numbers in each sequence. The alphabet has been written out to help you.

A B C D E F G H I J K L M N O P Q R S T U V W X Y Z

60 ACE   CEG   EGI   GIK   _____

61 BL   _____   DN   EO   FP

62	JIK	LKM	NMO	_____	RQS
63	546	555	564	573	_____
64	44	52	_____	54	48	56

5

If these words were placed in alphabetical order:

65 engine   excuse   engage   enamel   editor

Which word would be fourth? _____

B 20

66 motion   mirror   middle   millet   monkey

Which word would be first? _____

67 ledge   shove   house   level   shrub

Which word would be last? _____

3

A B C D E F G H I J K L M N O P Q R S T U V W X Y Z

B 24

If the code for PRIME is OQHLD, what is the code for the following word?

68 FOUR _____

If the code for KETTLE is JDSSKD, what does the following code stand for?

69 VQHSD _____

If the code for SECOND is QCAMLB, what are the codes for the following words?

70 PICNIC _____

71 HAT _____

72 SET _____

5

Read the first two statements and then underline one of the four options below that must be true.

B 25

73 'Cricket and football are ball games. Australians are very good at rugby and cricket.'

Australians play a game that uses a ball.

Cricket is played with a bat.

Australians are very good at football.

Rugby is played with a bat.

Read the first two statements and then underline one of the four options below that must be true.

74 'Turkey and mince pies are often eaten at Christmas. Turkey tastes good with cranberry sauce.'

Mince pies taste good with cranberry sauce.

Turkey is best with cream.

Cranberry sauce is sometimes served with turkey.

Cream is only eaten at Christmas.

Read the first two statements and then underline one of the four options below that must be true.

75 'Guitars are musical instruments. Guitars have strings.'

All musical instruments have strings.

All musical instruments need electricity.

Guitars are stringed instruments.

Strings are musical instruments.

Read the first two statements and then underline two of the four options below that must be true.

76–77 'Spanish and Italian are languages. Spain and Italy are in Europe.'

Spanish is a European language.

European languages are fun to learn.

Italians are Europeans.

People who speak Spanish also often speak Italian.

5

Underline the two words in each line which are most similar in type or meaning.

B 5

| **Example** | dear | pleasant | poor | extravagant | expensive |

78	flee	paint	exercise	retreat	drive
79	shoe	comb	eye	fur	coat
80	song	book	notice	law	message

3

Now go to the Progress Chart to record your score!   Total   80

Paper 13

Find the two letters which will end the first word and start the second word.

B 10

Example   rea (_c_ _h_) air

1 amu (__ __) ven

2 spo (__ __) ce

3 ste (__ __) ble

4 pro (__ __) rb

5 pri (__ __) dal

5

There are six houses in a street. They are arranged like this:

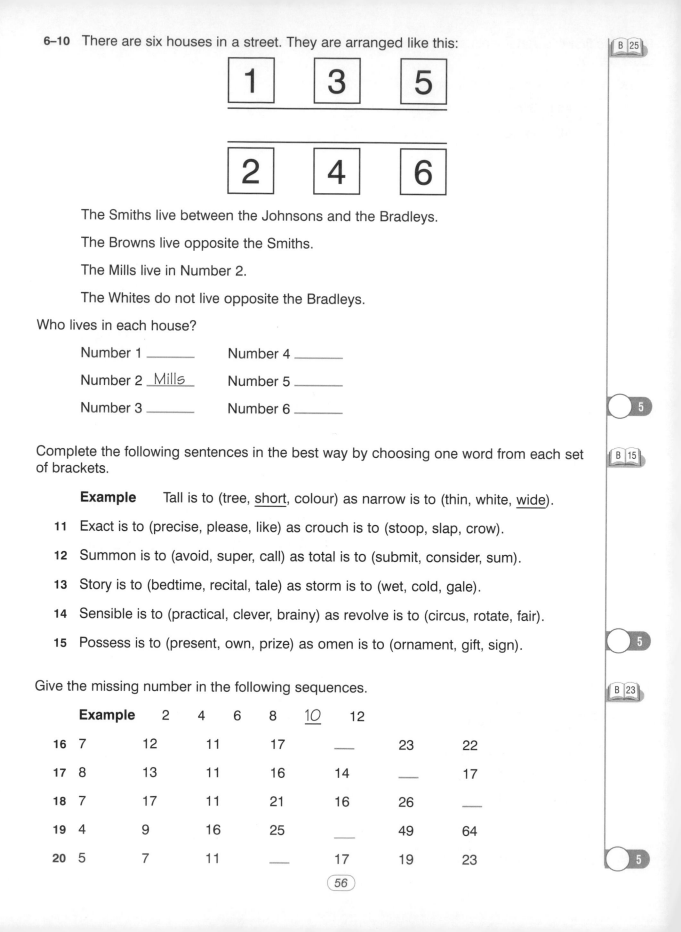

| 1 | 3 | 5 |

| 2 | 4 | 6 |

The Smiths live between the Johnsons and the Bradleys.

The Browns live opposite the Smiths.

The Mills live in Number 2.

The Whites do not live opposite the Bradleys.

Who lives in each house?

Number 1 _____   Number 4 _____

Number 2 _Mills_   Number 5 _____

Number 3 _____   Number 6 _____

Complete the following sentences in the best way by choosing one word from each set of brackets.

Example   Tall is to (tree, <u>short</u>, colour) as narrow is to (thin, white, <u>wide</u>).

11   Exact is to (precise, please, like) as crouch is to (stoop, slap, crow).

12   Summon is to (avoid, super, call) as total is to (submit, consider, sum).

13   Story is to (bedtime, recital, tale) as storm is to (wet, cold, gale).

14   Sensible is to (practical, clever, brainy) as revolve is to (circus, rotate, fair).

15   Possess is to (present, own, prize) as omen is to (ornament, gift, sign).

Give the missing number in the following sequences.

Example   2   4   6   8   <u>10</u>   12

16   7   12   11   17   —   23   22

17   8   13   11   16   14   —   17

18   7   17   11   21   16   26   —

19   4   9   16   25   —   49   64

20   5   7   11   —   17   19   23

A B C D E F G H I J K L M N O P Q R S T U V W X Y Z

If the code for HOLD is IPME, what is the code for the following word?

21 LOSE _____

If the code for PENCIL is QFODJM, what is the code for the following word?

22 LIP _____

If the code for FOOT is GPPU, what are the codes for the following words?

23 TOE _____

24 SUM _____

25 TOTAL _____

If A = 1, B = 2, C = 3 and so on, what is the sum of the following words if the letters are added together?

26 FACE = _____

27 BABE = _____

28 BACK = _____

29 HEAD = _____

Underline the one word in the brackets which will go equally well with both the pairs of words outside the brackets.

Example   rush, attack   cost, fee   (price, hasten, strike, <u>charge</u>, money)

30 touch, stroke   notice, sense   (feel, like, feign, hold, announce)

31 complimentary, gratis   untie, release   (charge, free, cost, nothing, loose)

32 armada, flotilla   rapid, fast   (fleet, short-lived, army, sea, float)

33 well, healthy   spasm, seizure   (fit, ill, old, shaky, unwell)

34 discover, reveal   bargain, windfall   (finish, find, luck, key, deal)

Find the four-letter word hidden at the end of one word and the beginning of the next word. The order of the letters may not be changed.

Example   The children had bats and balls   <u>sand</u>

35 The house was surrounded by a circular drive.   _____

36 The chosen few gathered around David.   _____

37 Edith sat in a cedar chair.   _____

38 Wait for him please at the top of the stairs.   _____

39 The tide appears to be receding.   _____

Change one word so that the sentence makes sense. Underline the word you are taking out and write your new word on the line.

B 14

Example   I waited in line to buy a <u>book</u> to see the film.   *ticket*

40 As I cut my birthday pie, I made a wish. _____

41 Please turn down your music, it's too soft. _____

42 The pilot told everyone to undo their seatbelts and prepare for take-off. _____

43 Dad was watching the six o'clock news on the radio. _____

44 Please wash your socks before coming to the dinner table. _____

5

A B C D E F G H I J K L M N O P Q R S T U V W X Y Z

B 24

If the code for EQUAL is GSWCN, what is the code for the following word?

45 BIRTH _____

If the code for MUDDLE is KSBBIC, what does the following code stand for?

46 DPGCLB _____

If the code for HUNDRED is LYRHVIH, what are the codes for the following words?

47 PICNIC _____   48 HAT _____   49 SET _____

5

Underline the one word in each group which **can be made** from the letters of the word in capital letters.

B 7

Example   CHAMPION   camping   notch   peach   cramp   <u>chimp</u>

50 PARLIAMENT   temper   plural   lemon   ailment   trait

51 DESCENDANT   scene   desert   second   tender   tandem

52 DELIVERANCE   render   cream   verge   driver   leader

53 TRIANGLE   elegant   grate   ranger   tingles   letter

54 DEALING   ailing   gleaning   ideas   nailed   landing

5

Solve the problem by working out the letter code. The alphabet has been written out to help you.

B 24

A B C D E F G H I J K L M N O P Q R S T U V W X Y Z

Example   If the code for SECOND is UGEQPF, what is the code for THIRD?   *VJKTF*

55 If the code for CLIMATE is IQMPCUE, what does SNVUQSS mean? _____

56 If the code for CROOKED is XILLPVW, what is the code for STRAIGHT? _____

57 If the code for BLISTER is DNKUVGT, what does UVKNG mean? _____

58 If the code for SMOOTH is UKQMVF, what is the code for HAIRY? _____

59 If the code for FACE is 6135, what does 85475 mean? _____

5

Find a word that can be put in front of each of the following words to make new, compound words.

Example	COST	FALL	WARD	POUR	DOWN
60 WRECK	MATE	YARD	SHAPE		_____
61 BELL	PRINT	BOTTLE	BERRY		_____
62 FINCH	FISH	MINE	SMITH		_____
63 BARROW	CHAIR	WRIGHT	SPIN		_____
64 FLY	FIELD	GROCER	HOUSE		_____

Fill in the crosswords so that all the given words are included. You have been given one letter as a clue in each crossword.

65–66

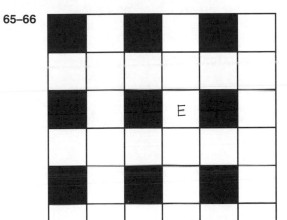

blasts, beasts, breeze, events, tennis, travel

67–68

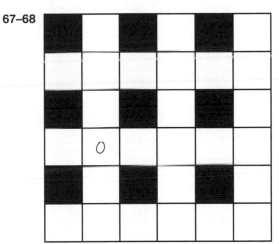

heaths, brakes, squeak, indoor, honest, unique

69–70

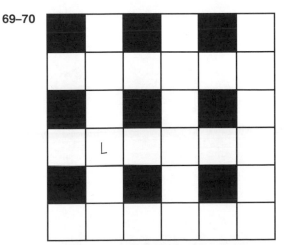

always, teaser, whiter, health, severe, depart

Underline the two words, one from each group, which are the most opposite in meaning.

Example   (down, <u>early</u>, wake)   (<u>late</u>, stop, sunrise)

71   (tall, narrow, jumping)   (slender, wide, bean)

72   (annoy, discomfort, reward)   (punishment, painless, distress)

73   (outcome, perfect, mistake)   (effect, flawless, flat)

74   (job, expensive, free)   (work, dear, enslave)

4

Write the words in each line in alphabetical order.

75–76	cushion	customary	culinary	culture	cupboard	curable
	_____	_____	_____	_____	_____	_____

77–78	precise	precious	pretty	previous	preen	precipice
	_____	_____	_____	_____	_____	_____

79–80	graphic	graph	gracious	grape	graphology	grapple
	_____	_____	_____	_____	_____	_____

6

Now go to the Progress Chart to record your score!   Total   80

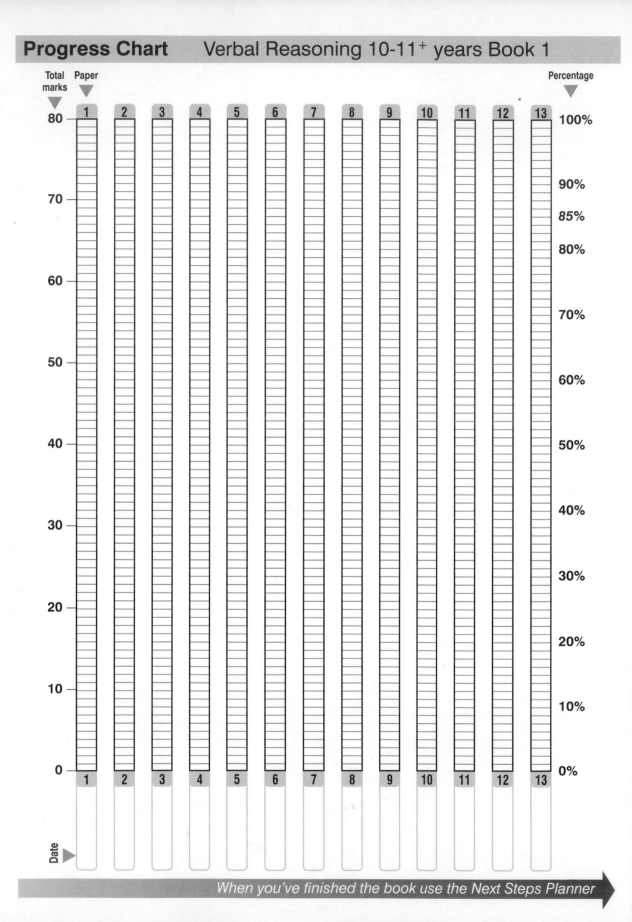

Progress Chart   Verbal Reasoning 10-11⁺ years Book 1

35 show
36 fort
37–40 *Give one mark for every three correct answers:* rainforest (B), passport (A), tempest (C), cotton (D), gale (C), tickets (A), visa (A), grassland (B), silk (D), mountains (B), tornado (C), wool (D)
41 THICKEN
42 TIED
43 REWARD
44 STRUNG
45 SOLVE
46 THUNDER
47 HEAD
48 TOOTH
49 HAND
50 FINGER
51 25, 33
52 59, 51
53 40, 160
54 11, 9
55 42, 9
56 RAT
57 OUR
58 ATE
59 MAT
60 OLD
61 C
62 A
63 B
64 B and C
65 B
66 built, bank
67 constructed, wall, markets
68 film, story, sad
69 fall, lengthened, set
70 hand, finger
71 two, double
72 hide, animal
73 happy, joy
74 pledge, promise
75 22
76 21
77 23
78 19
79 15
80 24

Paper 9

1 stick
2 clear
3 nail
4 deceive
5 stallion
6 ARCH
7 HERE
8 EVER
9 LAST
10 RAIN
11 sh
12 ch
13 lo
14 sh
15 le
16 DOLPHINS
17 PYRAMIDS
18 REPRODUCE
19 THATCHED
20 EMERGENCY
21 lifeless
22 setback
23 pipeline
24 outrage
25 afterwards
26 mile
27 stir
28 plight
29 spar
30 tire
31 ear, blink
32 clan, breathe
33 and, flake
34 one, dwell
35 spice, slide
36 some, sure
37 the, some
38 for, must
39 boy, name
40 soon, must
41 restore
42 portion
43 curb
44 puzzling
45 eject
46 CE, EK
47 ZA, QJ
48 KM, MI
49 BC, FG
50 UP, CL
51 AD, EH
52 34
53 19
54 82
55 15
56 245

57 CHIORST
58 N
59 CLAP, CLASP, CLEAN, CLING, CLOSE
60 face
61 cliff
62 4XA6
63 6XY6T
64 Y6XA6
65 ROWER
66 WOOL
67 Fire engines are red.
68 Ford make cars.
69 All wasps do not have bones.
70 You do not need bones to fly.
71 1.5 or $1\frac{1}{2}$
72 3
73 10
74 4
75 4
76 music, volume
77 sufficient, adequate
78 azure, navy
79 outfit, material
80 ear, eye

Paper 10

1 ALTER, LATER
2 SHRUB, BRUSH
3 CRATE, TRACE
4 STABLE, BLEATS
5 TOWELS, LOWEST
6 think, time
7 her, we
8 new, is
9 by, you
10 well, will
11 contradict, agree
12 guilty, innocent
13 reduce, increase
14 glut, insufficiency
15 divide, multiply
16 Sweets can be damaging to people.
17 Some rodents make good pets.
18 A reservoir provides water.
19 Henry was Elizabeth's father.
20 care

21 lukewarm
22 treasure
23 bake
24 stop
25 96, 91
26 72, 54
27 17, 19
28 6.66, 0.666
29 16, 18
30 soft
31 hats
32 bean
33 sent
34 rope
35 RAIN
36 LIGHT
37 DAY
38 WITH
39 BLACK
40 WELL
41 FLEE
42 RG2Z
43 X42Z
44 3X422ZX
45 forgive
46 guinea
47 quintet
48 interrupt
49 penalty
50 o
51 c
52 g
53 d
54 h
55 RAN
56 EAR
57 LAD
58 ALL
59 OUR
60 lace, pride
61 anger, dread
62 cease, frilly
63 lance, glisten
64 below, bridle
65 INFRTSI
66 AEVR
67 2534
68 SMALL
69 CDMKT
70 move, motion
71 overseas, abroad
72 over, under
73 peace, war
74 clear, lucid

75–80 *Give two marks for each correct crossword.*

'BLIGHT' and 'SLIGHT' are interchangeable in this crossword.

Paper 11

1 Houses are popular.
2 Houses need some form of heating.
3 Not all gardens are looked after.

4–7 *Give two marks for each correct crossword.*

8 cool
9 correct
10 bill
11 draw
12 claw
13 roundabout
14 somehow
15 justice
16 ballroom
17 spokesman
18 pen
19 foal
20 crowd
21 notion
22 join
23 l
24 a
25 e
26 t
27 k
28 start, term
29 be, l
30 for, love
31 paper, did

32 living, very
33 UKZVJ
34 HQWTVJ
35 EHQRS
36 EQNMS
37 AHFFDQ
38 0
39 0
40 10
41 91
42 5
43 twinkle
44 upset
45 titter
46 immense
47 minute
48 deliver
49 result
50 least
51 complete
52 late
53 trace
54 read
55 dear
56 tart
57 hatchet
58 mink
59 sole
60 slowing
61 rote
62 goal
63 RAIN
64 LIVE
65 SHIN
66 EASE
67 PENS
68 rain, told
69 bet, gain
70 plan, tent
71 mile, cosy
72 rust, cold
73 142
74 41
75 40
76 17
77 70
78 September
79 April
80 August

Paper 12

1 individual, different
2 crime, offence
3 value, worth

Bond Verbal Reasoning Assessment Papers 10-11+ years Book 1

Paper 1

1–5 *Give one mark for every two right*: clear B, sprouts D, fever A, ewe E, currant C, bean D, pony E, tanned B, damson C, cough A

6 warm
7 precise
8 complicated
9 hinder
10 last
11 sweet
12 flat
13 spot
14 mug
15 flag
16 d
17 t
18 k
19 n
20 e
21 SALAD
22 TRIANGLE
23 CIRCLE
24 SAUSAGES
25 WINTER
26 forgot
27 overtake
28 underground
29 fingerprint
30 below
31 rest
32 tall
33 here
34 hall
35 hero
36 LEND
37 BAIL
38 HOOT
39 COME
40 SAND
41 birds, flew, nest
42 climbed, bus
43 check, change, shop
44 footballer, kicked, pitch
45 elephants, long, trunks
46 there, wish
47 morning, get
48 hide, where
49 table, book
50 over, threw
51 NP
52 DFH
53 DW
54 OM

55 YS
56–59 *Give two marks for each correct crossword.*

T	A	P	E	R		B	E	A	R	S
A		I		I		R		C		U
S	E	E	D	S		E	A	T	E	N
T		C		K		A		O		N
E	V	E	R	Y		D	I	R	T	Y

60 EL
61 JI
62 VHS
63 OQP
64 pale, light
65 weapons, arms
66 right, correct
67 cushion, protect
68 MET
69 ATE
70 SEAT
71 TASTE
72 869934
73 pipe, heir
74 climb, ascend
75 hedgehog, porcupine
76 house, bracelet
77 biscuit, cake
78 5
79 16
80 1

Paper 2

1 NQ NS
2 NM OL
3 GR MX
4 7214
5 1425
6 5314
7 432
8 5327
9 picture, classroom
10 broke, vase, thrown away
11 caterpillars, butterflies, wings
12 times, you, door
13 rose, orange, ball
14 bandage
15 behind
16 birthday
17 foolhardy
18 colourless
19 miss
20 light
21 crib

22 lace
23 beam
24 h
25 k
26 w
27 l
28 t
29 AUTUMN
30 MANSION
31 ORCHARD
32 CRICKET
33 FERRET
34 men, draw
35 pump, land
36 lean, care
37 cave, cart
38 sea, bridle
39–43 *Give one mark for each two right answers:* turnip B, bugle A, adder C, drum A, cress B, snake C, piano A, onion B, tortoise C, guitar A
44 PUN
45 ARE
46 RED
47 LOW
48 BAD
49 rear
50 snow
51 reel
52 soft
53 lend
54 in, busy
55 bus, went
56 sums, do
57 cold, I
58 my, all
59–62 *Give two marks for each correct crossword.*

B	R	E	A	D		C	O	M	E	S
A		X		O		H		O		P
R	E	A	D	S		A	P	P	L	E
O		C		E		I		E		N
N	O	T	E	S		R	E	S	E	T

63 blue, sky
64 drink, thirst
65 girl, woman
66 high, low
67 soft, hard
68 6, 3
69 72, 24
70 29, 38
71 5, 38
72 15, 13
73 green

Bond Verbal Reasoning Assessment Papers 10-11+ years Book 1

74 red
75 1
76 four
77 BEAST
78 LOOP
79 FRAIL
80 NOTE

Paper 3

1 SHARES
2 SPRUCE
3 @ – × ÷ / %
4 % ÷ @ – £
5 × @ % ÷
6 <u>towels</u>, chips
7 <u>cream</u>, paint
8 <u>supermarket</u>, station
9 <u>ruler</u>, pencil or crayon
10 <u>door</u>, window
11 d
12 f
13 w
14 b
15 g
16 thing
17 shell
18 stop
19 whose
20 mire
21 kidnap, abduct
22 oil, lubricate
23 scarce, scanty
24 current, contemporary
25 flabbergast, astound
26 coast
27 dog
28 figure
29 goal
30 branch
31 dog, barked, lead
32 tower, view
33 forests, trees, animals
34 computer, information
35 quickly, play, puddles
36 dusk
37 fly
38 beach
39 twelve
40 green
41 refuse, offer
42 many, few
43 asleep, awake
44 ebb, flow
45 health, ailment

46 pencil, pen
47 believe, guess
48 horse, trough
49 road, rail
50 nephew, father
51 WITH
52 MASTER
53 AFTER
54 UP
55 NIGHT
56–59 *Give two marks for each correct crossword.*

60 18, 29
61 96, 36
62 38, 30
63 13, 13
64 4, 6
65 2 January
66 23 December
67 13 January
68 down
69 double
70 doubt
71 r
72 w
73 b
74 p
75 n
76 omen
77 scan
78 wink
79 term
80 here

Paper 4

1 REAL
2 NEST
3 FOUL
4 BEDS
5 TOOK
6 PEA
7 ONE
8 EAT
9 LAY
10 CAN
11 therefore
12 outlaw

13 inside
14 handsome
15 capable
16 reverse
17 wring
18 speak
19 peace
20 spoon
21 22
22 68
23 10
24 95
25 68
26 call, whisper
27 book, programme
28 face, leg
29 animal, house
30 skin, jelly
31 MQ
32 51
33 31
34 9
35 100
36 SOOTHE
37 CLOSE
38 LOST
39 ▼ ○ ■ ◆ ●
40 ○ ■ ◆ ▼
41 fire, ice
42 freeze, heat
43 night, morning
44 sea, land
45 toil, rest
46 faint
47 blow
48 charm
49 capital
50 break
51 ROLLING, MOSS
52 SEVEN, WEEK
53 COUNT, CHICKENS
54 CAPITAL, WALES
55 SEVEN, RAINBOW
56 XGJXF
57 HFMORTSG
58 CMVF
59 STUB
60 DUST
61–64 *Give two marks for each correct crossword.*

4 obtain, acquire
5 ordinary, normal
6 PART
7 ONCE
8 SIGN
9 TEAM
10 EARN
11 CROW
12 WARM
13 OARS
14 MARK
15 SOUR
16 e
17 k
18 b
19 d
20 p
21 bead
22 face
23 deed
24 eface
25 café
26 keyhole
27 nosedive
28 network
29 loudspeaker
30 outlook
31 vein
32 rest
33 twin
34 suet
35 sank
36 TRAY, TRAM
37 BENT, BEND
38 TRAP, TRIP
39 HOLE, HOLD
40 FAKE, FARE
41 book, couple, travelled
42 cheers, world, boat
43 rain, snow, ground
44 give, cause, worker
45 tidied, night, bed
46 window, table
47 she, got
48 far, think
49 us, you
50 done, nothing
51 start, begin
52 sight, sound
53 fib, honest
54 select, collect
55 talent, cure

56–59 *Give two marks for each correct crossword.*

A	S	P
S	I	R
S	P	Y

A	S	S
N	E	T
D	A	Y

60 IKM
61 CM
62 POQ
63 582
64 46
65 engine
66 middle
67 shrub
68 ENTQ
69 WRITE
70 NGALGA
71 FYR
72 QCR
73 Australians play a game that uses a ball.
74 Cranberry sauce is sometimes served with turkey.
75 Guitars are stringed instruments.
76 Spanish is a European language.
77 Italians are Europeans.
78 flee, retreat
79 fur, coat
80 notice, message

Paper 13

1 se
2 on
3 am
4 ve
5 me
6–10 1: Bradleys, 2: Mills, 3: Smiths, 4: Browns, 5: Johnsons, 6: Whites
11 precise, stoop
12 call, sum
13 tale, gale
14 practical, rotate
15 own, sign
16 16
17 19
18 22
19 36
20 13
21 MPTF

22 MJQ
23 UPF
24 TVN
25 UPUBM
26 15
27 10
28 17
29 18
30 feel
31 free
32 fleet
33 fit
34 find
35 lard
36 echo
37 arch
38 seat
39 idea
40 pie, cake
41 soft, loud
42 undo, fasten
43 radio, television or TV
44 socks, hands
45 DKTVJ
46 FRIEND
47 TMGRMG
48 LEX
49 WIX
50 ailment
51 scene
52 leader
53 grate
54 nailed
55 MIRRORS
56 HGIZRTSG
57 STILE
58 JYKPA
59 HEDGE
60 SHIP
61 BLUE
62 GOLD
63 WHEEL
64 GREEN
65–70 *Give two marks for each correct crossword.*

Bond Verbal Reasoning Assessment Papers 10-11⁺ years Book 1

71 narrow, wide
72 reward, punishment
73 mistake, flawless
74 free, enslave

Give two marks for each right answer:

75–76 culinary, culture, cupboard, curable, cushion, customary
77–78 precious, precipice, precise, preen, pretty, previous
79–80 gracious, grape, graph, graphic, graphology, grapple

65 baby
66 seedling
67 pushchair
68 letter
69 quadruple
70 People are not wood.
71 el
72 le
73 ge
74 al
75 re
76 your, where
77 need, pencils
78 some, I
79 at, like
80 day, dog

Paper 5

1 foe
2 heir
3 rough
4 calm
5 middle
6 milk, water
7 come, join
8 scales, feathers
9 you, me
10 odd, normal
11 block
12 fare
13 crop
14 post
15 mind
16 re
17 el
18 dy
19 on
20 le
21 bad
22 tease
23 matter
24 truce
25 stems
26 highlight
27 ringlet
28 farewell
29 overboard
30 crossbow
31 tour
32 soar
33 chin
34 seat
35 scan
36 lush
37 lair

38 mined
39 print
40 bride
41 car, lane, pedestrian
42 books, desk, lesson
43 pink, colour, scarf
44 scene, streets
45 darkness, thief, window
46 KO
47 DWE
48 KPD
49 HJH
50 LF
51 BEAR, BEAT
52 BAND, BANK
53 BALL, BELL or FELL, FELT
54 PATS, PASS
55 HULL, HALL
56–59 *Give two marks for each correct crossword.*

H	A	M		A	L	E
O	R	E		S	E	W
D	E	N		H	O	E

60 21, 57
61 8, 13
62 100, 79
63 saddle, tyre
64 east, west
65 grass, wall
66 cushion, needle
67 trumpet, nose
68 CAPE
69 ARE
70 = £ × × +
71 + × @ £
72 = £ @ + ÷ ×
73 RULE
74 PLASTER
75 PLEASE
76 TRUST
77 OCEAN
78 25
79 29
80 16

Paper 6

1 29
2 24
3 17
4 33
5 46

6 FALSE
7 NEAR
8 TRACE
9 BRUSH
10 TABLE
11 PHRASE
12 real
13 hats
14 they
15 tool
16 fort
17 trellis, roses, pruning
18 book, exciting
19 drummed, car roof, school
20 savage, postman, letters
21 day, water, plants
22 le
23 ch
24 sh
25 ic
26 en
27 EI
28 VO
29 786
30 568
31 19
32 rival, opponent
33 spine, backbone
34 sure, certain
35 bluff, pretend
36 brave, fearless
37 NEST, TENS
38 STEP, PEST
39 LEAP, PALE
40 WEST, STEW
41 LAIR, RAIL
42 in, was
43 was, when
44 brave, was
45 into, sieved
46 start, will
47 CHEAT
48 ACHE
49 TRACE
50 ● ■ ○ ◗ ~
51 ○ ■ ● ▮
52 TAR
53 EAR
54 TON
55 OAR
56 CUT
57 cupboard
58 crossword

59 foreground
60 deadlock
61 forgive
62 tarnished
63 boisterous
64 speak
65 starving
66 midway
67 Anne
68 Emma
69 fencing
70 tap dancing
71 two
72 LAKE, LIKE
73 PILE, PILL
74 WOOD, WORD
75 HOPE, ROPE
76 WART, MART
77 FATTEN (4), LIGHTEN (2), MOISTEN (3), SOFTEN (1)
78 COMICAL (1), FINAL (4), MUSICAL (2), OFFICIAL (3)
79 CATCHMENT (3), FITMENT (4), ODDMENT (1), SEGMENT (2)
80 DANCING (1), CRYING (4), FLYING (3), SAYING (2)

Paper 7

1 SEND, DENS
2 LAST, SALT
3 LAPSE, SEPAL
4 ADDER, DREAD
5 POST, STOP
6 rust, trend
7 rose, place
8 font, rice
9 clan, plane
10 eat, bend
11 push, in
12 tilt, level
13 egg, seed
14 cherish, question
15 destroy, discover
16 6844
17 3824
18 6851
19 3844
20 LAWS
21 mallet
22 flexible
23 ravenous
24 entire
25 cleanse

26 holidays, birthday
27 cat, dog
28 soldier, queen
29 picture, book
30 newts, tadpoles
31 ADD
32 TAN
33 TAR
34 RAN
35 HER
36 63, 42
37 50, 56
38 4, 32
39 20, 10
40 100, 45
41 st
42 ch
43 ch
44 ed
45 en
46 7316
47 CKBMLDU
48 UQHV
49 SPLASH
50 NWOR
51 pupil
52 commence
53 loosen
54 descend
55 hide
56 PAPER
57 COUNTER
58 UNDER
59 HEAD
60 SEA
61–66 *Give two marks for each correct crossword.*

S	P	A	R	E		S	T	A	L	E
O		C		A		U		W		V
L	A	T	E	R		P	E	A	C	E
I		E		L		E		I		N
D	A	D	D	Y		R	A	T	E	S

D	I	M	L	Y
R		E		E
O	P	E	R	A
N		T		R
E	A	S	E	S

67 FURNACE
68 FUSS
69 FURROW
70 FUSE
71 FURNITURE

72 Emily
73 Trigger
74 Willow
75 Beauty
76 Halo
77 Tuesday, it
78 room, leave
79 four, is
80 fur, silk

Paper 8

1 trap, snare
2 let, allow
3 too, also
4 bowl, dish
5 watch, survey
6 too, your
7 may, think
8 at, you
9 her, got
10 on, the
11 4552
12 3526
13 8546
14 5784
15 NURSE
16 PEAK
17 MOAN
18 SEAL
19 PORT
20 TURN
21–26 *Give two marks for each correct crossword.*

27 te
28 el
29 in
30 le
31 or
32 hero
33 rent
34 wash

A4